Theory for Theatre Studies: Sound

Online resources to accompany this book are available at https://bloomsbury.com/theory-for-theatre-studies-sound-9781474246460. Please type the URL into your web browser and follow the instructions to access the Companion Website. If you experience any problems, please contact Bloomsbury at: contact@bloomsbury.com.

Theory for Theatre Studies meets the need for accessible, mid-length volumes that unpack keywords that lie at the core of the discipline. Aimed primarily at undergraduate students and secondarily at postgraduates and researchers, volumes feature both background material historicizing the term, and original, forward-looking research into intersecting theoretical trends in the field. Case studies ground volumes in praxis, and additional resources online ensure readers are equipped with the necessary skills and understanding as they move deeper into the discipline.

Series editors

Susan Bennett, University of Calgary, Canada
Kim Solga, Western University, Canada

Published titles

Theory for Theatre Studies: Space

Kim Solga

Forthcoming titles

Theory for Theatre Studies: Movement Rachel Fensham
Theory for Theatre Studies: Emotion Peta Tait
Theory for Theatre Studies: Economics Michael McKinnie
Theory for Theatre Studies: Memory Milija Gluhovic

Theory for Theatre Studies: Sound

Susan Bennett

Series editors:
Susan Bennett and Kim Solga

methuen | drama
LONDON • NEW YORK • OXFORD • NEW DELHI • SYDNEY

METHUEN DRAMA
Bloomsbury Publishing Plc
50 Bedford Square, London, WC1B 3DP, UK
1385 Broadway, New York, NY 10018, USA

BLOOMSBURY, METHUEN DRAMA and the Methuen Drama logo
are trademarks of Bloomsbury Publishing Plc

First published in Great Britain 2019

Copyright © Susan Bennett, 2019

Susan Bennett has asserted her right under the Copyright, Designs and
Patents Act, 1988, to be identified as the author of this work.

For legal purposes the Acknowledgements on p. ix constitute
an extension of this copyright page.

Series design by Louise Dugdale
Cover image © Henrik Sorensen/Getty Images

All rights reserved. No part of this publication may be reproduced or
transmitted in any form or by any means, electronic or mechanical,
including photocopying, recording, or any information storage or retrieval
system, without prior permission in writing from the publishers.

Bloomsbury Publishing Plc does not have any control over, or
responsibility for, any third-party websites referred to or in this book. All
internet addresses given in this book were correct at the time of going
to press. The author and publisher regret any inconvenience caused if
addresses have changed or sites have ceased to exist, but can accept no
responsibility for any such changes.

A catalogue record for this book is available from the British Library.

A catalog record for this book is available from the Library of Congress.

ISBN:	HB:	978-1-4742-4646-0
	PB:	978-1-4742-4647-7
	ePDF:	978-1-4742-4645-3
	eBook:	978-1-4742-4648-4

Series: Theory for Theatre Studies

Typeset by Integra Software Services Pvt. Ltd.
Printed and bound in India

To find out more about our authors and books visit www.bloomsbury.com
and sign up for our newsletters.

For Barnaby,
maestro of sound

CONTENTS

Acknowledgements ix
Series Preface x

Sound: An Introduction 1

SECTION ONE
Classical Sound 15

Theatres in ancient Greece and Aristotle's *Poetics* 15
The vocal map of ancient Greek drama 18
Vitruvius on acoustics: *De Architectura* 24
Shakespeare's Globe and Francis Bacon's *Sylva Sylvarum* 27
Acoustic world-making on the early modern stage 35
A sonic imagination of early modern London 48

SECTION TWO
Avant-Garde Sound 53

New technologies for sound performance 53
Hanging on the telephone: Sigmund Freud and Roland Barthes 63
The sounds of silence: John Cage's future of music 70
Acousmatics and radiophonics: Pierre Schaeffer and the BBC 78
Aura and archive: Making sound memories 85

SECTION THREE
Experiential Sound 97

Prosthetic performance and deterritorialized listening 97
Listening to women: Andrea Hornick and Luce Irigaray 107
Affective theatres of embodied sound 113
Coda: Sound across the world 128

References 132
Further Reading 142
Index 145

ACKNOWLEDGEMENTS

I start with warmest thanks to Kim Solga, my co-editor in putting together this series: she agreed with alacrity to explore the possibility of these *Theory* volumes and since then has proven time and again an energetic collaborator and astute colleague as we have written our own two texts and commissioned authors to write others. Her unfailing enthusiasm for student learning and her relentless pursuit of fair and equitable pedagogies make us all better not only in our classroom practices but also in thinking more carefully about those we write for and how.

Sincere thanks are due, too, to Mark Dudgeon and his team at Bloomsbury. Mark has been a champion of this series from its inception, and he continues to provide thoughtful and generous support in its development. Lara Bateman has done a terrific job in ensuring authors, including this one, stay on track and are well informed about the Bloomsbury publication process.

I am grateful to the Faculty of Arts at the University of Calgary for a six-month Research & Scholarship Leave during which time the first draft of this book was worked out. But, even more importantly, *Sound* would not have found its voice without the opportunity to teach a graduate seminar on interdisciplinary sound studies and the wonderfully rich discussions that the students in this class fostered each week. The podcasts this group of students produced at the end of the course were without exception dazzling in their intellectual range, as well as rigorous, innovative and often moving. Their work inspired this work. Much love, always, to my family – it is a perennial joy to share their creative worlds.

SERIES PREFACE

Theory for Theatre Studies (TfTS) is a series of introductory theoretical monographs intended for both undergraduate and postgraduate students as well as researchers branching out into fresh fields. It aims to introduce constellations of ideas, methods, theories and rubrics central to the working concerns of scholars in theatre and performance studies at the opening of the twenty-first century. With a primary focus on twentieth-century developments, TfTS volumes offer accessible and provocative engagements with critical theory that inspire new ways of thinking theory in important disciplinary and interdisciplinary modes.

The series features full-length volumes explicitly aimed at unpacking sets of ideas that have coalesced around carefully chosen key terms in theatre and performance, such as space, sound, bodies, memory, movement, economies and emotion. TfTS volumes do not aggregate existing essays, but rather provide a careful, fresh synthesis of what extensive reading by our authors reveals to be key nodes of interconnection between related theoretical models. The goal of these texts is to introduce readers to a wide variety of critical approaches and to unpack the complex theory useful for both performance analysis and creation.

Each volume in the series focuses on one specific set of theoretical concerns, constellated around a term that has become central to understanding the social and political labour of theatre and performance work at the turn of the millennium. The organization of each book follows a common template: Section One includes a historical overview of interconnected theoretical models, Section Two features extended case studies using twentieth- and twenty-first-century performances and

Section Three looks ahead, as our authors explore important new developments in their constellation. Each volume is broad enough in scope to look laterally across its topic for compelling connections to related concerns, yet specific enough to be comprehensive in its assessment of its particular term. The ideas explored and explained through lively and detailed case studies provide diverse critical approaches for reading all kinds of plays and performances as well as starting points for practical exploration.

Each book includes a further reading section, and features a companion website with chapter summaries, questions for discussion, and a host of video and other web links.

Susan Bennett (University of Calgary, Canada)
and Kim Solga (Western University, Canada)

Sound: An Introduction

Sitting on the bus, walking across campus to class, travelling on a plane, working out at the gym and so many more everyday scenarios where thought, action and even perhaps sense of self are now typically accompanied by a soundtrack. It has become a commonplace to go through the day with headphones in ears, listening to a curated playlist, favourite radio channel, podcast, audio book or a randomized selection of music housed on a personal Apple or other branded mobile device. As fans of theatre, we may be subscribed to the 'PlayMe' podcast, 'transforming drama for the digital age' and allowing us to listen to original 'Canadian Indie Theatre on a national and international scale' (Expect Theatre). Often, of course, we choose a soundtrack to serve a purpose – change or set a mood, inspire an activity, provide us with street directions or just to block out the more unsettling and unwelcome sounds of daily life, especially those of a city such as traffic, machinery, too many other people. We live in a sound world that regularly serves as a barrier to noise pollution in the real world. Michael Bull describes our immersion in sound as an 'audiotopia', created by the 'intense pleasure' and 'desire for continuous, uninterrupted use' of iPods (2011: 528). More materially, Trevor Pinch and Karin Bijsterveld note that sound has been rendered '"thing-like" – a commodity to be bought and sold on iTunes, a thing to be worn, as with personal stereos' (2012: 5).

Even without headphones deployed, our daily lives are pervaded and distracted by music and other varieties of ambient sound, part of a contemporary experience of elevators, stores, coffee shops and restaurants, gyms, hotel lobbies, art installations and so on. We are subjects hailed by these public space soundtracks, chosen not (or, at least, not just) to entertain us but more explicitly to put us in a mood conducive to shopping or eating or working out. Sometimes a soundtrack – often made up of classical music or opera – is designed and deployed to discourage us from lingering too long at a particular site (many public transit authorities have used this strategy). This plethora of everyday sound experiences Anahid Kassabian has usefully captured for us as 'ubiquitous listening' (2013: 40).

The number and variety of these commonplace sonic engagements make up a narrative of 'human-technology coupling', David Cecchetto would say (2013: 4), and it is hardly surprising that so many theorists have started to examine 'the sonic turn' of the twenty-first century. How do we understand the ways sound shapes theatrical production and reception? How have sonic practices informed the performances we make or attend? This book aims to think through the many elements of sound that inform theatre and performance and to provide critical entry points for engaging the breadth of theory across historical and disciplinary perspectives concerned with the nature of sound. Scholarship in theatre and performance studies for a very long time emphasized, sometimes almost exclusively, matters of visuality and of embodiment, even as it was recognized that sound in its various forms is an intrinsic part of any performance experience. It has long been obvious, after all, that audiences receive a great deal of information, not to mention enjoyment, through what they hear from the stage as much as from what they see. Gertrude Stein, way back in 1935, declared, 'I say nothing is more interesting to know about the theatre than the relation of sight and sound' (1957: 113). To this end, *Sound* will look at different theories and diverse performances that have explored and articulated how various sonic elements shape and inform theatrical production and reception.

While this book will explore critical discussions of the role of sound in theatrical production, it will also look at theoretical writing about sound more broadly and via cognate disciplines so as to measure the usefulness of this work for investigations of performance matters. With careful attention to relevant period studies that have thought through sound in specific historical contexts, as well as to key disciplinary and interdisciplinary texts, *Sound* will engage a wide range of theatre and performance examples as well as provide case studies so as to model a sound focus and methodology. But how, exactly, should we think of this topic of sound? As a starting point, then, let's take up Mark Grimshaw's definition: '*Sound is an emergent perception arising primarily in the auditory system and that is formed through spatio-temporal processes in an embodied environment*' (2017: 468, italicized in original).

What Grimshaw emphasizes is the relational nature of sound: we understand it through space, time and the body (all areas that have been amply theorized within theatre and performance studies). Also, we might note that he begins with an emphasis on the 'auditory system' and, thus, pays attention to the role of the listener. Grimshaw amplifies his gloss as follows:

> The definition also stresses the importance of perceptual context and opens the door to an understanding of the dynamic relationship between sound and memory, experience, imagination, affect, and cross-modality. Thus, sound really is all in the mind and its emergent perception is formed from varying combinations of material, sensuous stimuli (possibly, but not necessarily, sound waves) or immaterial, non-sensuous phenomena (such as imagination and memory). (2017: 469)

Theatre director Peter Sellars, like Grimshaw, ties sound to memory: 'That is to say, sound is where we locate ourselves, not physically, but mentally and spiritually. Sound exists inside our heads. It is our greatest experience of intimacy. It transports us' (1992). Hans-Thies Lehmann, in his oft-cited account of 'postdramatic theatre', calls for an 'independent *auditory semiotics*' (2006: 91, emphasis in original). And Lynne Kendrick asks us to think through 'theatre aurality', 'a mode of engagement that – because it cannot be captured by the eye – can exceed the boundaries by which our visible world is marked out for us ... sound can redraw the spaces and environments around us' (2017: xxii). In this book, we will explore a range of sound experiences and consider how production elements impact and affect audiences.

Sound is, in the sonic sense, a sampling. The goal of the book is to generate key questions and productive approaches that will encourage students and researchers to conduct their own investigations of sound in the theatres and performances they value. To this end, what should we consider as sound in a theatrical context? The term catches within it elements such as voice, music and song, sound effects, soundtracks, intended and unintended noises (what Mladen Ovadija calls 'environmental onstage and offstage events' [2016: 11]), acoustics, resonance, noise and even silence – many of these fully deserving of a theoretical study of their own and certainly all in need of careful explication and historicization. We might think, for example, that the category of sound effects is both transparent and transhistorical – what is the storm at the beginning of Shakespeare's *The Tempest* but a remarkable sound effect? But, in fact, this sonic term came into use only in the twentieth century in the infancy of the Hollywood film industry, the *Oxford English Dictionary* (*OED*) providing the word's first citation from a 1909 advertisement in *Moving Picture World* for the makers of 'high grade sound effects.' The *OED* does, however, include the theatre in its annotation of common usage: 'a sound typical of an event or evocative of an atmosphere, produced artificially in a play, film, etc.', suggesting how this modern concept has been taken up multimodally and made retroactively applicable to discussions of theatrical practice at any historical moment.

Sound in the theatre also implies – indeed, requires – listening. Audiences, by virtue of their presence, are contracted to listen and, inevitably, become producers of sound themselves (some intended: clapping, laughing and so on; others less so: coughing, chatting and so on). Actors onstage and the technical crew offstage are all equally contracted to acts of listening – to each other and for feedback. Remember, too, that the etymology of audience connects the term specifically to hearing and that the *OED* defines an audience primarily as a body of hearers ('All the people within hearing of something; (hence) the assembled listeners or spectators at a public performance or event'). How audiences listen is one area of the theatrical sound experience that has generated thorough and lively scholarly attention. Ross Brown, for example, has argued that listening at a performance is 'focused hearing – active auditory attention that attends to one thing at a time or follows a particular, "monophonic" flow (which might be an ensemble of sounds)' (2010: 135–6). Yet, that 'focused hearing' cannot ever be fully realized as Rey Chow and James A. Steintrager point out: 'even when we attend to a sound's source, we sense sound as an emanation and as filling the space around us. Objects as sonic phenomena are points of diffusion that in listening we attempt to gather' (2011: 2). Sound's tendency is always towards the immersive.

With this in mind, George Home-Cook writes that there is 'a great deal more to listening than meets the ear' and suggests even as 'the listener resides *in* the medium of sound, equally this medium must be attended, explored and travelled through. In short: listening, as an intersensorial act of stretching, involves paying attention to atmospheres' (2015: 168–9). His work refines the idea of a focused listening directed at sonic phenomena so as to produce what he calls aural attention. He suggests that how we perceive by way of listening in the theatre is, in fact, 'an inter-subjective act of embodied participation' (2015: 168). Home-Cook's approach is principally phenomenological – a way of thinking that we will look at again later in the section on 'avant-garde' sound (through a discussion of French theorist Pierre Schaeffer's concept of acousmatics and Samuel Beckett's radio play *All That Fall*). That listening can demand active or passive participation is also considered by critic and composer Michel Chion. He likewise employs a phenomenological framework in which to elucidate these modes of response. Where our eyes can only focus on a single point, our ears, Chion contends, hear everything: 'There is always something about sound that overwhelms and surprises us no matter what – especially when we refuse to lend it our conscious attention; and thus sound interferes with our perception' (2012: 53). From the first theatres of ancient Greece to the most recent genres of performance, the production of sound and the ways we hear/listen/attend aurally have formed a dynamic network that we now strive to better describe.

Particularly challenging for theatre studies scholars is the task of listening to performances from the past. J. L. Stoever warns: 'Sounds disconnected from their contexts of reception rarely answer our questions about the past, but merely make for new listening experiences in the present' (2009). This argument notwithstanding, Bruce Smith has proposed that when we look to recover sound in performances from earlier periods, we should become 'acoustic archaeologists who "un-air" sounds that have faded into the air's atmosphere and catalogue them' (2004: 22). The first section of *Sound* starts with such a project – how to listen to the theatres, and the sound theorists, of ancient Greece and early modern England, to consider how acoustics were practised and understood in those times and to rehearse our archaeological skills. An acoustic archaeologist might take as her task the construction of a 'soundscape' – a term first coined in the 1970s to describe all the sounds that make up a particular environment. To make a soundscape that described a performance from the past, then, we would want to consider not just those sounds created by and in a particular production but also those that somehow and necessarily contextualize it. As well, we would need to recognize the assumptions we bring to bear on building that soundscape: in effect, we would need to comprehend and elucidate our own sonic (listening) histories.

Theatrical sound has, of course, long been a subject of considerable interest for technical study of the theatre, and practices of sound production have been extensively and usefully explored in the context of stage design. Ross Brown's *Sound: A Reader in Theatre Practice* provides a valuable introduction to 'designing sound in relation to dramaturgy' (2010: xiii), and this work includes a useful survey of textbooks in the field from across the twentieth century. Deena Kaye and James Lebrecht's *Sound and Music for the Theatre: The Art and Technique of Design* is one of the best-known and highly regarded manuals for the would-be sound designer. The authors warn the reader that '[a]s a sound designer, you may encounter the perplexed looks of others as they wonder what exactly sound design is. Tell them that sound design is the creative and technical process resulting in the complete aural environment for live theatre – just like the music and sound accompanying film' (2013: 1). What follows in their volume is a detailed workthrough from concept to running the show. Notwithstanding the emergence of sound design as a significant professional field, theatre sound as a critical enquiry was long consigned to a background role, rarely doing more than support the main action of performance research. We might look here at Patrice Pavis's practical text *Analyzing Performance* (2003) where one of his ten chapters is devoted to 'Voice, Music, Rhythm'. For the first of these three terms, Pavis suggests that 'the voice is also a projection of the body into the text, a means of making the corporeal presence of the actor felt' (2003: 140). Music he limits to 'how it serves the theatrical event' and rhythm as what 'organizes speaking bodies moving in the time-space of a stage' (2003: 140, 145). In other words, he shifts the impacts of voice, music and rhythm to serve those categories we have historically privileged in our studies of theatre – time, space and embodiment – at the same time as he omits or at least ignores other common performance elements such as sound effects, sound scores and other varieties of sonic intervention.

More recently, however, there has been much more interest in elaborating the work of sound in theatrical performance. Less than a decade after publication of *Analyzing Performance* (in English), for example, the collection *Theatre Noise: The Sound of Performance* (2011) set the stage for more complex examinations conducted across a range of theatrical styles and performance genres, where Pavis, here as author of the book's Foreword, moots 'Is it sound's turn?' (x). The book's editors certainly thought it was, but elect to make a move from sound to noise, explaining that their term 'captures an agitatory acoustic aesthetic. It expresses the innate theatricality of sound design and performance, articulates the reach of auditory spaces, the art of vocality, the complexity of acts of audience, the political in produced noises' (2011: xv). In their definition of theatre noise, the editors looked to suggest the textured vocabulary that discussions of sound, in performance and in the world, employ.

Burgeoning interest in the complex terrain of sound as a primary meaning-making mode in theatre and performance – how it works socially, politically, ethically and psychologically – has been informed by and resonates with the rapid expansion in the twenty-first century of the field of Sound Studies, an area marked by the publication of two hefty anthologies in 2012. In *The Sound Studies Reader*, Jonathan Sterne introduces Sound Studies as 'a name for the interdisciplinary ferment in the human sciences that takes sound as its analytical point of departure or arrival' (2012: 2) and further explains that scholarship in the area looks 'to think across sounds, to consider sonic phenomena in relationship to one another ... whether they be music, voices, listening, media, buildings, performances, or another other path into sonic life' (2012: 3). Even as 'performance' appears as a term within Sterne's list of sonic categories, we should recognize that all the other elements in his string bear examination in thinking about sound in theatre.

In the other field-defining collection, editors Trevor Pinch and Karin Bijsterveld introduce *The Oxford Handbook of*

Sound Studies with the observation that 'sound is no longer just sound; it has become technologically produced and mediated sound' (2012: 4). They call for new sonic skills with which to listen (2012: 11). Both volumes mark the need to counteract the hegemony of the visual ('ocularcentrism') and seek to rebalance scholarly interests between what we see and what we hear. Two years earlier Gustavus Stadler, introducing a Sound Studies issue of the journal *Social Text*, argued that the field's interdisciplinary interests provide ways to 'reassess and replenish political critique. What matters here is learning how to hear what power, history, culture and difference sound like' (2010a: 10–11). Sterne makes much the same case when he insists that investigations of sound 'attend to the (cultural, political, environmental, aesthetic ...) stakes of that knowledge production' (2012: 3–4, ellipses in original). *Sound* will look to keep these stakes in view across the historical and theoretical scope of the book.

While much of Sound Studies scholarship is directed towards the latest technological conditions of sound production and potential acts of listening ('new sonic skills'), Sterne's work looks back to the history of sound. His scholarship has echoes of Smith's acoustic archaeology, suggesting that sound is 'at different moments strangely silent, strangely gory, strangely visual, and always contextual. This is because that elusive inside world of sound – the sonorous, the auditory, the heard, the very density of sonic experience – emerges and becomes perceptible only through its exteriors' (2003: 13). Thus we cannot authentically recover 'an auditory past' but must instead focus on 'the social and cultural grounds of sonic experience' (Sterne 2003: 13) or, as French social theorist Jacques Attali puts it, 'it is sounds and their arrangements that fashion societies (2012: 31)'. Simply put, sound has always been (and continues to be) crucial to the production and circulation of power.

Roland Barthes concluded his treatise on listening (a work that we will examine in more detail in the second section of this book, 'Avant-Garde Sound') with a claim for its potential to resist: 'no law is in a position to constrain our listening: freedom of listening is as necessary as freedom of speech' (Barthes 1985: 260). He celebrated the 'sonic imagination' of the audience. But while listening may be liberatory, being listened to conjures much darker possibilities. Attali ventures: 'Eavesdropping, censorship, recording, and surveillance are weapons of power. The technology of listening in on, ordering, transmitting, and recording noise is at the heart of this apparatus' (2012: 32). Twenty-first-century performances have often examined exactly this relationship between sound and surveillance; in Section Three, we will look at Rimini Protokoll's *Situation Rooms*, a performance that equips audience-participants with headphones to act out precisely these kinds of conditions.

Sound follows a three-part structure that moves chronologically through history. This arrangement recognizes that to think about sound – and certainly to think about sound in theatre and performance – is to recognize an evolution of knowledge about how sounds are made and heard. New technologies of sound production and reception generate new theories that systematize the new practices. At the same time, new technologies inspire new subjects for and innovative modes of delivery in performance. This book addresses the span of sonic history in the theatre.

The first section of *Sound* will explore theories of sound as part of a canonical Western tradition. We will look at what key thinkers have had to say about sound in the theatre as well as how we think this might have been experienced in performance. Starting with the earliest drama of ancient Greece, we will consider ideas about sound in the context of the period with particular attention to places of production (such as the theatre at Epidaurus and, later, at Shakespeare's Globe) and to relevant sonic practices (such as music, sound effects and textual cues). This account of 'classical sound' is not a survey of dramatic theory or of sound design, but rather it looks at the theatres of ancient Greece and of early modern England in order to think about how theatres have employed sound at particular historical moments and how theorists, both contemporary to these periods and since, have understood the matter of their sound production. Two case studies, of Aristophanes' *The Frogs* and Shakespeare's *The Tempest*, will allow us to explore how sound features work in their respective periods as well as to take up how the plays' soundscapes have been adapted for later audiences.

The second section will turn to 'avant-garde sound' to address a fascination with and dependence on emergent technologies of sound production in the late nineteenth century and through to the mid-twentieth century. It will look first at the theatrical experiments of the Italian Futurists and the fervour with which they met the modern city and all of the sounds it generated. Because of their excitement in and fascination for the new possibilities of making and hearing sound, the Futurists often not only undertook the elucidation of new theoretical perspectives but also revelled in the making of sound-saturated performances.

'Avant-garde sound' is also concerned with the new machineries of sound – developments in communications engineering – and how these inventions changed both sound production and what Grimshaw calls 'the dynamic relationship between sound and memory, experience, imagination, affect, and cross-modality' (2017: 469). We will look, too, at how these inventions found their way into theories of performance as well as emerged as contributors to stage practice. A case study of Italian Futurist Luigi Russolo's orchestra of intonamuri will examine how noise and silence entered a sonic performance vocabulary – a topic that will be further developed in a discussion of John Cage's imagination of the 'future of music'. Two further case studies, of Jean Cocteau's *The Human Voice* and Samuel Beckett's *Krapp's Last Tape*, will allow us to consider the impacts, on stage and in the audience, of specific technological developments: the telephone and the tape recorder.

The final section will examine 'experiential sound', a reflection on performance practices that envelop the spectator in a curated and participatory soundscape made possible by the development of mobile sound technologies. Looking at two of Canadian artist Janet Cardiff's audio/video projects ('Forest Walk' and 'The Telephone Call'), we will examine how new portable devices – in the first example, the Sony Walkman and in the second, a small digital camera – took sound performance (and its audiences) out of the theatre building into other performance spaces. 'Experiential sound' relies on the availability of headphones, an apparatus that Michael Bull describes as transforming 'the users' relationship to the environment' and creating 'sonic privacy' (2011: 529) – their adoption proliferating to the extent we now recognize a genre of 'headphone theatre'. Case studies will look at how oral histories, delivered through mobile technology, become sonic experiences that aim to compel their listeners to empathize with, and sometimes (re-)enact, those narratives. In this section, we will examine Shannon Yee's *Reassembled, Slightly Askew*, a headphone drama about the author's experience of a devastating illness and recovery, and Rimini Protokoll's *Situation Rooms*, a peripatetic sonic adventure that asks its audience-participants to encounter the extraordinarily diverse conditions and impacts of the global arms trade. 'Experiential sound' will address the common assertion that active listening converts sound into memory.

A coda to this final section will ask questions about the application of this book's theoretical scope to those sonic elements that do not originate in Western ways of thinking about sound matters or in Western conventions of sound design for performance.

Whether researching theatre as a critic or a practitioner, a beginner or an expert, *Sound* alerts us to the possibilities of knowing more about this vital element of performance. It insists that we think further about how sound in theatre and performance works in the social, cultural and political moments in which it is produced and heard. The ideas and examples that follow are intended to help with what Gertrude Stein saw as the axiomatic puzzle of her theatregoing experiences: 'Does the thing heard replace the thing seen. Does it help or does it interfere with it' (1957: 101).

SECTION ONE

Classical Sound

Theatres in ancient Greece and Aristotle's *Poetics*

The history of Western theatre starts in Greece and the history of 'Western theatrical theory essentially begins with Aristotle' (Carlson 1993: 15). And both the ancient theatres and Aristotle's theory are important to this project about sound. They remind us that the first theatres were predominantly aural and that the first theory was attentive to the production of sound theatrically as well as to the effects on the audience it sought to create.

Perhaps the best-known example of the earliest theatre buildings is the amphitheatre at Epidaurus, built in the fourth century BCE and since 1988 a UNESCO World Heritage site. Its excellent preservation has allowed us to learn – as well as to speculate – about theatre practices in the classical period. Epidaurus can accommodate as many as 14,000 spectators. Its vast size means that spectators in the back row find themselves more than 60 metres from the playing area, yet the theatre is famous for its extraordinary acoustics. The actor's voice, even at a whisper, can be heard at any point on any row. A landmark essay in *The Journal of the Acoustical Society of America,* published in 2007, revealed what its authors, Nico F. Declercq and Cindy S. A. Dekeyser, call 'the geometry of the theater' and how this might explain such an exemplary capacity to carry sound (2007: 2012). Thus, these researchers had set out to understand, by measuring across different frequencies, how 'sound behaves after interaction with the seats of the theater' (Declercq and Dekeyser 2007: 2012). They concluded that 'the seat rows act like a filter' (2007: 2021), effectively muzzling background noise at the same time as the limestone-constructed rows boost the sounds emanating from the playing area. Modern acoustical science, then, was able to disprove a long-held myth that the clarity with which sound travelled at Epidaurus might be explained by frequent local winds; in fact, the scientists' experiments found that, acoustically, those winds often had a negative effect on the theatre's immaculate sound (Declercq and Dekeyser 2007: 2012).

If the seat rows at Epidaurus were a boon to a sound-based theatre, the wearing of masks by the actors on the ancient Greek stage was almost certainly an inhibition. Today's theatre spectators know how valuable variations in facial expression can be as interpretive cues and how a mask denies this familiar and productive interaction and, moreover, the use of masks, whether in contemporary or ancient Greek theatres, also constrains engagement between actors themselves since mask design is necessarily forward facing. Studies of images of masked actors on ceramics of the same period in ancient Greece – there are no actual masks extant – suggest that their sight holes were no larger than the human eye, requiring 'the act of *akroasis*, the act of conscious and active listening' for actors and audience alike (Kontomichos 2014: 1445). Furthermore, distances between the actors and at least the spectators in the upper levels of the sharply raked rows undoubtedly meant that the performers would have appeared almost in miniature for those farthest away.

With the substantial limitations imposed on what we now think of as conventional theatrical relationships (between actors and audience as well as between actor and actor) created by the visual dimensions of acting, sound was everything. For this reason, Edith Hall has described Greek tragedy as 'a palette of vocal techniques with which to paint ... sound pictures' (2002: 7); Graham Ley argues that the genre 'relied heavily on the voice' (2006: 54) and required 'three kinds of vocal delivery', speaking, chant and singing (2007: 83). Theatrical performances traded on the knowledge and skill of audience members at the City Dionysia, an annual festival of drama and song, since many of the Athenian men and boys who came to see the plays would also have been participants in the festival's choral competitions. The playwrights recognized their audience as 'experienced, even expert, in recognizing and assessing various poetic and musical styles and skills, especially in regard to the choral parts – rhythms and melodies; choreography; clarity and tunefulness of singing' (Griffith 2013: 115–16) and were able, therefore, to craft their plays for these sophisticated ears. As Mark Griffith summarizes, 'Athenian culture in general was highly musical, and the theatregoers were probably more so than average' (2013: 116).

In this context, it is interesting to see what Aristotle's *Poetics*, the genesis document for Western theatre theory, has to say about sound. Although best known for its definition of the dramatic genres, much of Aristotle's attention in *Poetics* goes specifically to tragedy, 'an action of a superior kind' (2013: 23), which he asserts has six elements, listed from the most important to the least: 'the story, the moral element, the style, the ideas, the staging, and the music' (2013: 24). His more detailed description of the components of tragedy does not put a great deal of stock in staging, saying it 'can be emotionally attractive, but is not a matter of art and is not integral to poetry' and music comes last in his taxonomy (2013: 25). Yet, at the same time, Aristotle insists that 'music is the most important source of pleasure' (2013: 25) and, later in the *Poetics*, he returns to music in espousing an argument about the inferiority of epic when it is compared with tragedy: 'there is nothing that epic has that tragedy does not also have – it can even use the same metre – but tragedy has a substantial extra element in the form of music, which is a source of intense pleasure' (2013: 55). Unfortunately, Aristotle does not give us any further account of how exactly music might incite such pleasure nor does he elaborate on the importance of pleasure for the spectator of Greek tragedy. But it is useful to remember this turn to the affective power of sound in this earliest reference text for theorizing theatrical practices.

The *Poetics* also describes the structure of tragedy: 'prologue, episode, finale, and chorus parts (sung either on entry or while stationary). These items are common to all plays; some have in addition arias and dirges' (2013: 31). Aristotle goes on to explain this arrangement in terms that emphasize the crucial organizing function of the chorus:

> A prologue is everything in a tragedy that precedes the opening chorus; an episode is whatever comes between two complete choral songs; and the finale is everything that comes after the final chorus. Of the choral part, the opening chorus is the first complete utterance of the chorus; while a stationary ode is a choral song without anapaests or trochees. A dirge is a lament shared between the chorus and the actors. (2013: 31)

Theory in the *Poetics* therefore suggests that the action of Greek drama was produced by highly formal and elaborately layered sonic elements. The actors provided oratory but the chorus and musicians added the sounds (and movement) that turned words into drama for an audience whose sonic knowledge was already expert.

The vocal map of ancient Greek drama

In his discussion of the theatricality of Greek theatre, Ley proposes that the text of a Greek tragedy is better understood as 'a vocal rather than just a semantic script, a composition directing a variety of implementations of the capacities of the human voice' (2007: 84). And it was through the vocal map of a play that character differentiation was produced and action created with the different Greek playwrights each deploying sound to specific and particular purpose. In Aeschylus's plays, the chorus often drives the action of the play in both word and song (for example, in their role of searching for Orestes in the *Eumenides*) (Ley 2006: 69–71) and in *Agamemnon*, Cassandra is described as singing like a nightingale. In Sophocles's plays, the central male character generally sings to indicate an emotional apex (Hall 2002: 7). In Euripides' plays, the chorus is regularly employed in singing and chant, both to orchestrate stage action and to provide the audience with guiding commentary. As Simon Goldhill explains, 'the chorus mobilizes the *voice of the community* – with the full weight of what community means in democracy and in the shared cultural world of the ancient city' (2007: 50); in other words, the varieties of sound that a chorus employs work collectively not simply to give representation to the citizens in the audience but to participate in the production of democratic identity, often doing so from a particularly marginalized position (for example, a chorus of women). This sense of the chorus as community holds both potential and appeal for contemporary productions of Greek tragedy although how to translate its repertoire of sound for the twenty-first century is, as Goldhill says, 'most vexing' (2007: 45).

In 1965 Roland Barthes had made a similar point about performances of Greek drama, deliberating on why modern adaptations so often aim for authenticity when 'we frequently perform Shakespeare today without bothering about the Elizabethan conventions' (1985: 87). He asserts that 'reconstruction is impossible', because of incomplete knowledge, 'notably with regard to the plastic function of the chorus, which is the stumbling block of all modern productions' (1985: 87). How to handle the music is, he suggests, equally fraught: 'Greek music was monadic, the Greeks knew no other kind; but for us moderns, whose music is polyphonic, all monody becomes exotic: hence a fatal signification, which the ancient Greeks certainly did not want' (1985: 88). As outlined in the Introduction, theorization of sound concerned with theatres of the past inevitably challenges us to elaborate its qualities and contributions in the context of our own sonic histories and experiences of listening. Thus we are obliged to weigh what kinds of sonic adaptation are necessary, appropriate and/or effective when reading or producing a play that is not a contemporary one and whether knowledge of the original conditions of sound realization is relevant, informative or a barrier to the possibilities of a play's new life.

That the chorus of Greek drama was accompanied by music, usually *auloi* (a reeded double pipe) and sometimes lyre (stringed instruments), adds to sense that performance comprised more a musical score than a play text. *Auloi* were 'particularly prominent in connection with *choroi* [the chorus]' and the sound these flutes created was 'for want of a better, general term, piercing' (Ley 2007: 133). Imagine, then, the arrival of the chorus singing, dancing and accompanied by the arresting screech of the *auloi*, a fully sonic transition between prologue and the main action of the play. For Peter Wilson, '[b]y far the most important and intimate relationship' in Greek tragedy was the one between musician and chorus (2002: 39). But without sufficient evidence to reconstruct the vocal register of the choruses or the melodies of the music that accompanied them, it is obviously a challenge to know how to make either work effectively in a contemporary staging of Greek tragedy (whether attempting an original practices performance or a modern adaptation). Wilson makes the important point that a 'tune on the most authentically reconstructed *aulos* is, in isolation, almost as meaningless to the modern ear as a recitation of a speech of Euripides to someone ignorant of the structure of ancient Greek' (2002: 41) – a problem for the scholar of historical sound, to be sure, and an issue to which this book will return on several occasions.

But Wilson does not see this as the only, or even the most vexatious, difficulty; rather, he points out that Aristotle's dismissal of staging ('not a matter of art'), along with the ranking of music as the least important of his six elements of tragedy, has created a bias that informs how scholars of ancient Greek theatre attend to sonic contributions. Instead of focusing almost singularly on extant text, we need as much to remember how frequently playwrights and theorists of the period privileged sound, song, music and melody in their writing for and about theatre. As Barthes insisted, we have a responsibility to rediscover 'the rigorous distinction of the spoken, the sung, and the declaimed, or the massive, frontal plasticity of the chorus ... its essentially lyric function' (1985: 88). Notwithstanding the considerable challenges attached to the revivification of sound from ancient plays as well as Barthes's combination of cautions and recommendations, a much-admired production of Aeschylus's *The Suppliant Women* by The Actors Company (2016–17) resurrected the use of *auloi* in a new score for the play composed by John Browne – an element that marketed the ancient instruments as 'heard on stage for the first time in 2500 years'! The *auloi*-infused soundtrack was employed to frame the involvement of fifty local women (not actors) who served as a contemporary-day chorus of refugees seeking asylum, a choice that reviewer Allan Radcliffe described as producing a 'truly hypnotic effect' (2016).

Case study: Aristophanes' *The Frogs*

Like the earlier tragedies, Aristophanes' eleven plays (the only extant evidence of 'old' Greek comedy) demonstrate a sophisticated deployment of sound – vocal styles, music, singing and so on. Of particular interest to this study is *The Frogs* (written around 405 BCE) where, in one of the play's comic episodes, Aristophanes pits Aeschylus against Euripides as to who wrote superior tragedies: an onstage 'battle' between the actors in these roles that requires them to sing parodies of each other's work. In Aristophanes' play, Dionysus – the god whose festivals, the City Dionysia, were the inspiration for the first Greek drama – finds himself unhappy at the state of contemporary playwriting. He travels to Hades to find Euripides (who had only recently died) and finds there the dramatist in competition with Aeschylus as to who is the better playwright. Upon his arrival, Dionysus is asked to judge. What follows is an extended parody of both Aeschylus's and Euripides' styles, intended to entertain the audience as brilliantly comic pastiche. But their rendition of each other's work also provides an illuminating historical document for better understanding the sonic techniques characteristic of the two earlier writers. After Aeschylus and Euripides have each made a case for the qualities of their prologues, Dionysus asks them to address lyrics – to which Euripides quickly replies, 'His lyrics are all the same' (Aristophanes 1964: 201). Euripides' ennui with Aeschylus's writing is then demonstrated by the former's performance of lyrics from eight of Aeschylus's plays. As Mark Griffith has pointed out, *The Frogs* reveals Aeschylus's songs to 'adhere quite closely to a venerable Panhellenic performance tradition' (2013: 133) and, since only one of the eight performance pieces is taken from an extant play (*Agamemnon*), Aristophanes' play furnishes additional historical evidence for the rhythms and structures of Aeschylus's choral odes across his oeuvre (see Griffith 2013: 133).

The Frogs is equally useful for its laying out of the very different Euripidean soundscape. In response to the critique of his own compositional style, Aeschylus produces a pre-prepared parody of Euripides' lyric that he performs to the accompaniment of a dancing girl – an additional (visual) gesture that succinctly indicates Aeschylus's poor opinion of his opponent. In this performance, Euripides' lyrics veer away from traditional patterns 'in favour of "free," non-strophic stanzas of unpredictable metrical character' (Griffith 2013: 137). As Griffith explains, this shows the 'much more vocal and instrumental bravura' of Euripides' works that 'form part of a decisive shift in the structure and character of Greek drama during the later fifth century' (2013: 137). The extended exchange is obviously designed to poke fun at both the traditionally styled lyric compositions of Aeschylus, described most frequently by the Chorus and Dionysus as examples of 'good' writing, and the more modern and 'free' style of Euripides, chiefly admired for the 'cleverness' of his work. That Aeschylus is finally declared the winner is not point; rather, *The Frogs* demonstrates Aristophanes' own bravura in composition.

But *The Frogs* has also proven to be an important resource for scholars concerned with a fuller historical understanding of how the earliest Greek dramas sounded. The Aeschylus–Euripides contest at the heart of the play has also, provocatively perhaps, been identified as one of the earliest examples of the stage musical. Given this critical assertion, it is perhaps less surprising to discover that Stephen Sondheim was commissioned to prepare a new version of *The Frogs* in 1974 'as an after season fund-raising lark, staged in the Yale [University] swimming pool' (Brustein 2004: 25). The Yale Repertory Theatre production is legendary, chiefly for having had both Meryl Streep and Sigourney Weaver in its cast. But, in thinking about 'classical sound', the Sondheim version is notable by way of its shift from discovery of Aeschylus and Euripides sounding off in Hades to more recent (and English-speaking) playwrights, William Shakespeare and George Bernard Shaw, in competition. In Sondheim's version, Shakespeare rather than Aeschylus emerges triumphant (fortune favours tradition, it seems) after 'singing the first two stanzas of "Fear no more" from *Cymbeline* (the *only* time in Sondheim's career that he has set someone else's lyrics)' (Gamel 2007: 218). This adaptation of *The Frogs* was revived in 2004 by Nathan Lane, in a New York City production (at the Vivian Beaumont Theatre), directed by Susan Stroman and set in an explicitly post-9/11 context.

If The Actors Company's *The Suppliant Woman* made a persuasive case for the effectiveness of *auloi* in a contemporary interpretation, these two productions of *The Frogs* involving Broadway luminaries such as Sondheim, Lane and Stroman suggest that the integral place of sound in the earliest dramas is not so much lost as ready to be reimagined in new ways for the audiences of their times.

Vitruvius on acoustics: *De Architectura*

While Declercq and Dekeyser's study of the theatre at Epidaurus could not prove that it was designed and built with a working knowledge of what shape, size and materials would produce the near-perfect acoustics (it could have simply been 'a coincidence' [2007: 2011]), the subject of sound in the theatre had nevertheless become fully theorized some two hundred years later. Marcus Vitruvius Pollio's ten-book treatise *De Architectura* (*Of Architecture*), written in the first century BCE, gives considerable attention to the principles of construction for public buildings in general and theatres in particular. *De Architectura* is generally considered to be Vitruvius's compilation of 'best practices' rather than a manifesto of his own invention, but it remains a significant source since it is the only text we have that outlines the theory behind classical architecture. The importance of a theatre building to the public spaces of Roman culture is signalled when Vitruvius puts it second only to the construction of the forum (1999: 65). Chapter 3 in Book 5 of *De Architectura* is devoted to this particular topic. After brief instructions about site selection, Vitruvius spells out in detail the form required for an amphitheatre:

> It seems that the transverse aisles of theaters should correspond in their dimensions to the total height of theaters, and in no case should the heights of the backs of the aisles exceed their breadth. If they are made higher, they will repel the voice, casting it out of the upper part of the theater; in the upper seats, those above the aisles, such theaters will not allow the endings of words to reach the ears of the listeners distinctly. In short, determine the height

like this: if a line is extended from the lowest step to the highest, it should touch the edge of every step, that is, every angle. In this way, the voice will not be obstructed. (1999: 65–6)

De Architectura describes the variations in construction methods between Greek and Roman theatres and pays attention to the distinctive acoustical properties of site selection. 'Dissonant' sites are 'those in which the voice first rises high, then meets resistance from solid surfaces higher up, and when it is deflected back it comes to rest low, preventing the rise of any other sounds' (1999: 70). 'Dispersive' sites create a lack of clarity and 'resonant' sites produce echoes, but 'consonant' sites are those where the voice 'reaches the ears with precise clarity' (1999: 70). The superiority of the consonant site for theatrical performance is elaborated at some length:

The voice is a flowing breath of air, and perceptible to the hearing by its touch. It moves by the endless formation of circles, just as endlessly expanding circles of waves are made in standing water if a stone is thrown into it. These travel outward from the center as far as they can, until some local constriction stands in the way, or some other obstacle that prevents the waves from completing their patterns .... For the voice, therefore, just as for the pattern of waves in water, so long as no obstacle interferes with the first wave, it will not upset the second wave or any of those that follow; all of them will reach the ears of the spectators, without echoing, those in the lower-most seats as well as those in the highest. (1999: 66).

Here Vitruvius returns to 'the architects of old' (1999: 66) – that is, the builders of the first Greek theatres – and suggests that they used 'the canonical theory of mathematicians and the principles of music' to calculate how to most effectively build 'on harmonic principles to amplify the voice' (1999: 66).

Chapter 4 offers a description of the principles of Greek harmonics and, in Chapter 5, Vitruvius employs these principles to advise on the use of the *echea*, bronze vessels dispersed between the seats in a theatre employed to clarify and amplify the voices on stage. He includes technical detail on the placement of *echea*, suggesting, helpfully, that smaller theatres 'in towns of no great size' (1999: 68) can produce similar effects but with a much cheaper option, clay jars. Vitruvius also deals with the wooden, rather than stone, theatres that were proliferating in Rome at the time, explaining that the floors provide the necessary resonance and no *echea* are required. In his explication of theatre design, Vitruvius mentions the convention of 'a clap of thunder' that accompanies 'the epiphany of a god' (1999: 69), a brief reference to a sound effect that David Collison links to earlier evidence that the Greek theatres may have had stage machinery for this single purpose (2008: 7, 8).

By the first century BCE, then, theatre building had become codified, organized to optimize sound. As part of this practice, a preliminary acoustical science developed so as to meet the defining condition for successful play performance: accuracy in hearing for all spectators. With theatres recognized as fundamental to the development of Greek and then Roman towns and cities, a theory of sound to describe effective delivery from stage to audience was inevitable. The relationship between sound, architecture and audience thus defined the first Western theatres and, in fact, every theatre since that time. Moreover, Vitruvius's *De Architectura* was an immensely influential text in the Italian Renaissance and was referenced by English architects in the mid-sixteenth century (although it was not in fact translated into English until the end of the seventeenth century). Acoustical theory, then, has a long history that informed choices in design and construction materials for theatre buildings, and experimentation in the sound capabilities of performance spaces has long brought about systematized practices in production and reception, elaborating how distinctive sonic features contribute to the theatrical experience.

Shakespeare's Globe and Francis Bacon's *Sylva Sylvarum*

As public and private theatres were developed and designed in late sixteenth- and early seventeenth-century England, proximity between stage and audience might suggest that sound need not predominate their construction principles in the ways that it had for the ancient auditoria. But, whether open air or indoors, the theatres of early modern London were also acoustically sophisticated spaces that the early modern playwrights and the newly formed theatre companies sought to exploit. After all, descriptions of theatregoing in the period describe audiences going to hear a play rather than see it (Escolme 2016: 107).

'Authentic' reproduction projects such as Shakespeare's Globe (opened in 1997) and the indoor Sam Wanamaker Theatre (opened in 2014) on the south bank of the River Thames in London as well as the American Shakespeare Center's Blackfriars Playhouse in Staunton, Virginia (2001), have allowed for academic research and performance experimentation that attempts to theorize precisely how sound might have worked in those buildings and what audiences might have heard. Claire van Kampen, for example, has written of the 'aural texture' of the replica Globe, recognizing how its architecture put the theatre's musicians on show – an emphasis on their importance for and within the performance of a play:

> The music gallery, or 'room,' being placed directly above the stage, in the centre of the *frons scenae*, is at the most powerful visual point in the stage picture. What is more, in an 'original practices' production, musicians are dressed in Elizabethan clothing, which is colourful, far from the standard black uniform of the modern performer. ... In the

present Globe reconstruction, the music gallery completes the middle circle, which, unlike the upper and lower gallery, runs all the way around the stage. For 'original practices' productions, audiences were therefore seated on either side of the music gallery, in the lords' rooms, thus being behind the stage itself, on the line of the *frons scenae*. (Interestingly, from this position, audibility of the text is increased, though visibility of the action is reduced.) (2008: 81)

Interesting, indeed, that the most expensive seats in the theatre – those in the lords' room – were the best for attending to sound. Bruce Smith observes, 'In terms of both vision and hearing, the Lords' Room offered an optimal situation: one could not only see and be seen but hear and be heard: the canopy [over the stage] would have projected the lords' voices as well as the actors' (1999: 214). (Rather than opposing van Kampen's assertion of less visibility from the Lords' Room, Smith's observation about sight lines is directed, I think, more towards looking at the audience than viewing the stage.) Van Kampen also explains that the location of the musicians telegraphed to early modern theatregoers the place of the Muses, between heaven and earth, with the effect that music at the Globe was 'not only heard but **seen** as the expression of the Muses as it transmits heavenly impulses to Man below on the earthly stage' (2008: 81). These examples illustrate the coupling of sound and sight that fostered meaning not just for the play in performance but also for the social relationships within the audience.

Attempts to recapture the sonic experience of early modern performance do not, however, originate with the building of these replica theatres in the late twentieth and early twenty-first centuries. Arnold Dolmetsch, a French-born instrument maker whose workshop was in Surrey (England), collaborated with William Poel in the early twentieth century on all the influential director's productions of Shakespeare's plays and Dolmetsch is considered one of the most significant figures in the revival of early music practices (see Lindley 2008: 91).

Internationally recognized, the Academy of Ancient Music (AAM) has been singularly committed to the production of 'original' period sound since the ensemble's founding in the early 1970s. AAM set out to retrieve the 'essence' and 'spirit' of baroque music through a return to original production methods: 'strings made of animal gut, not steel. The trumpets had no valves. The violins and violas didn't have chin rests, and the cellists gripped their instruments between their legs rather than resting them on the floor' (Academy, n.d.). In other words, the principles of the AAM's sound practice were based on authentic period-specific instruments and original technologies for playing them, a commitment to historical accuracy much like *auloi*-playing incorporated in the 2016–17 production of *The Suppliant Women*. These practices might seem to afford musicians and audience alike a kind of time travel to the past but such a possibility has always been contentious. Arguments against attempts to reproduce 'original' conditions either in the concert hall or on the stage insist that hearing in the twenty-first century is inescapably filtered by the history, sonic and otherwise, that exists between earlier periods and the present. Contemporary audiences may simply not connect to, or even understand, an 'original' production component because of its difference from what is now conventional. As David Linley rightly insists, we cannot 'get unmediated acoustic access to Shakespeare's world, no matter how historically informed the musical performance may be' (2008: 97) – the ways we hear stage music are shaped inevitably by our familiarity with much more recent genres of music and, particularly perhaps, film and television soundtracks.

In a related context, Paul Meier reminds us that if we could find ourselves at the very first production of *Hamlet*, 'we would understand little of what the actors have to say' because of radical differences in how words were pronounced (2016: 179). How early modern actors spoke Shakespeare's words and how audiences heard them is at the heart of experimentation with Early Modern English (EME) pronunciation more commonly referred to as original pronunciation (OP). To investigate how EME/OP pronunciation would impact performance, Shakespeare's Globe invited David Crystal, a linguistics professor specializing in this area, to collaborate on an EME/OP production of *Romeo and Juliet* in 2004. Crystal's book *Pronouncing Shakespeare* is his story of that project. An EME production of *Troilus and Cressida* followed in 2005. Crystal writes that the consensus among the actors and other theatre personnel was that the 'audiences were totally engaged' (2005: 136) and he quotes Tom Cornford, then an assistant director at Shakespeare's Globe: 'What OP has revealed to me is the extent to which Shakespeare's language "bodies forth" his characters' (2005: 144). Crystal's son, Ben, an actor, makes the same point in a YouTube demonstration of EME pronunciation – that it requires a much more physical performance and that it speeds up delivery of the lines, suggesting why a play in Shakespeare's time might have been but 'two hours traffic on the stage' (as the Prologue to *Romeo and Juliet* has it) rather than the considerably longer running time typical of contemporary productions of his plays (Open 2011). Deploying the sound of early modern English also reveals 'lost rhymes, puns and wordplay' (Meier 2016: 180), opening up the text, paradoxically, to new meanings and interpretation.

Experimentation with differently sounded English has the effect, then, of drawing attention to conventions of Shakespearean acting – what we hear, for example, when a Royal Shakespeare Company (RSC) actor delivers a speech and how we might be reminded that this is not the 'natural' or 'authentic' sound of Shakespeare's words but a way of speaking learned by actors and expected by the RSC's audiences. Thus, EME productions of Shakespeare ask sonic questions beyond the performances on the Globe's stage to any and all productions of historically remote drama: for example, how have words, whether Shakespeare's or another writer's, become speech in a particular historical moment and what were the conventions of delivery at that time? Certainly, the work of David and Ben Crystal has been instrumental in emphasizing what had perhaps seemed an apparently irretrievable gap between sounds that were made on an early modern London stage and how they were heard in the audience. They ask us to consider what 'original' or 'authentic' pronunciation (and, for that matter, other 'original' or 'authentic' elements) might open up for original practices productions and their audiences today. Even if contemporary spectators necessarily hear through their own sonic histories (see the Introduction to this book), the commitment of institutions like Shakespeare's Globe and the AAM to attempt historically authentic sound tempers the authority claimed by some original practices productions where the concept is realized predominantly, if not exclusively, by elements belonging to the visual register of performance.

However successful or not, however useful or not, a return to past technologies of performance might be, it is simply impossible for a contemporary audience to listen as audiences several hundred years ago would have. For this reason, among others, critics in both musicology and theatre studies have challenged the term 'original practices': Lydia Goehr, in a survey of the critical arguments about the early music movement, outlines a move to 'a multiplicity of ways to be authentic' (2007: 283) while Don Weingust has argued for 'historically informed performance' as a much more accurate term: 'One might well ask whether any theatrical or other artistic practice can be anything but a practice of its present' (2014: 410). These kinds of criticism are just as true for reception, giving rise to the commonsensical point so often made about the experience of original practices productions at Shakespeare's Globe where the very modern interruptions of planes and helicopters flying over the theatre are inevitably part of a spectator's sonic experience. Such anomalies extend to even more mundane interventions such as the chirps and songs of birds that land on the playhouse roof or on the stage – some of these birds are species that would not have been native to London in the sixteenth or seventeenth centuries.

Yet, even if we cannot hear as an early modern spectator would have done, we do know a great deal about how sound was generated and understood in early modern England. This is among the subjects addressed in Francis Bacon's *Sylva Sylvarum: Or, A Natural History in Ten Centuries*, a work published posthumously in 1651 by his personal secretary William Rawley. Although the text postdates Shakespeare's career as a dramatist, and indeed the playwright's death, *Sylva Sylvarum* is nonetheless useful for capturing the sense of mystery that had surrounded the production and reception of sound in early seventeenth-century England. Among many and varied interests in this volume, Bacon examines how sound operates and carefully charts distinctions between visual and aural fields of representation.

Bacon's project in *Sylva Sylvarum* is to account for all of life on earth through an extensive range of experiments, the premises and proofs for which he proposes in some detail. No modern edition of *Sylva Sylvarum* exists, but facsimile texts are easily found in print and online. In the quotations that follow, I have generally modernized spelling and punctuation for ease of reading. Note, also, that the book's organization in 'ten Centuries' reflects a rare use of 'Century' that the OED explains as a particular volume in a larger history, a definition that is supported by various citations from sixteenth- and seventeenth-century ecclesiastical histories.

At the outset of Century II, Bacon argues that in the case of music, practice has been ably explained, 'but in the theory, and especially in the yielding of the causes of the practique, very weakly, being reduced into certain mystical subtleties of no use, and not much truth' (1651: 29). So, in lieu of mystery, he looks to develop a taxonomy of sound. Bacon examines sounds in nature (rain, wind and so on); the voices of humans, beasts and birds; and music. In each case, he proposes a series of experiments to explain their causes and their effects. Many of these experiments require specific properties (often domestic, such as glass, wood and musical instruments) to illustrate a technically detailed acoustics. For the human voice, Bacon offers physiological explanations. But it is in the following volume, Century III, that he elaborates the operations of sound in terms that might well have been inspired by his experience of early modern performance and even a knowledge of how sound was understood in the construction of the period's theatres.

In the first sentence of Century III, Bacon asserts that '[a]ll sounds (whatsoever) move Round, that is to say on all sides: upwards, downwards, forwards, and backwards. This appears in all instances. Sounds do not require to be conveyed to the sense, in a right line as visibles do, but may be arched' (1651: 49) – something that not only recalls the acoustical theories behind the ancient Greek theatres but also describes architectural principles that informed the polygonal structure of the Globe theatres. Bacon offers a description of how sounds travel, what they can penetrate and what causes them to be muffled. To contrast visual and aural effects, he points out that colours 'when they represent themselves to the eye, fade not, nor melt not by degrees, but appear still in the same strength; but sounds melt, and vanish, little by little' (1651: 51). As sounds 'melt' and 'vanish', so does live performance and, remarkably, we find that Shakespeare relied on the very same verbs to describe the dissipation of the wedding masque in *The Tempest*: a stage direction indicates that the singing masque performers '*heavily vanish*' (4.1.138 SD) and Prospero tells its audience, Ferdinand and Miranda, 'Our revels now are ended. These our actors, / As I foretold you, were all spirits and / Are melted into air' (4.1.149–50).

Further, Bacon extends his analysis to the condition of listening to sound. Thus Century III also considers the cognitive processes behind reliable hearing and again draws attention to differences between how people understand what they see and how they process what they hear:

> There is an apparent diversity between the species, visible and audible, in this: that the visible does not mingle in the medium, but the audible does. For if we look abroad, we see heaven, a number of stars, trees, hills, men, beasts, at once.

And the species of the one does not confound the other. But if so many sounds come from several parts, one of them would utterly confound the other. So we see that voices or consorts of music do make a harmony by mixture, which colours do not. ... a great sound drowns a lesser. (1651: 53)

Human inability to separate a mixture of sounds into its constituent parts while, at the same time, possessing the more efficient capacity to process a number of different visual signifiers requires explanation: 'Sight works in right lines and makes several cones and so there can be no coincidence in the eye, or visual point. But sounds that move in oblique and arcuate [*OED*, citing *Sylva Sylvarum*, "curved like a bow"] lines must needs encounter and disturb the one the other' (1651: 53). Experience of the many public performances of early seventeenth-century culture (those in theatre, of course, and also other kinds of contemporary practice such as royal processions, public hangings and ballads sung on street corners) would have informed Bacon's theoretical principles for how sound moves in space and how humans process it, particularly in combination with visual images. In other words, his is a performance-based comprehension.

In fact, when Bacon shifts to matters of the human voice and its delivery, he offers two examples that draw directly on theatrical practices. In one, he is concerned with a capacity and intention to imitate another speaker: 'we see that there are certain "pantomimi" that will represent the voices of players of interludes so to life, as if you see them not, you would think they were those players themselves' (1651: 56). He does not elaborate on whether this kind of sound production creates good entertainment or whether it simply produces anxiety in the hearer in the possibility of being duped through vocal imitation, but his description suggests there was a buoyant market for impersonation of celebrity actors. Additionally, this illustration recalls the particular concern of early seventeenth-century Puritans – that impersonation was a dishonest medium, likely to lead to fraudulent behaviour and the duping of innocent parties.

The suggestion of deceptive activity comes in another of Bacon's examples where he refers to skill in the manipulation of voice and, in particular, the talent to project so that what is said appears to come from elsewhere:

> There have been some that could counterfeit the distance of voices (which is a secondary object of hearing) in some sort, as when they stand fast by you, you would think the speech came from far off, in a fearful manner. How this is done may be further enquired. But I see no great use of it, but for imposture, in counterfeiting ghosts or spirits. (1651: 56)

While Bacon finds this ability perhaps too trivial to explore in more depth, his notion of its very limited utility might well derive from the popularity of ghosts and spirits on the early modern stage (consider Andrea in Thomas Kyd's *The Spanish Tragedy*, a popular sixteenth-century play revived regularly into the early seventeenth, or the ghost of old King Hamlet in Shakespeare's tragedy).

Before moving for the balance of Century III to a new set of experiments that might explain the duration of a human life, Bacon summarizes his theorization of sound: 'We have laboured … in this inquisition of sounds, diligently, both because sound is one of the most hidden portions of Nature (as we said in the beginning) and because it is a virtue which may be called incorporeal and immaterial, whereof there be in Nature but few' (1651: 23). In other words, of all the experiments that *Sylva Sylvarum* works through, Bacon found sound among the most challenging, not the least because of its intrinsic ephemerality.

Acoustic world-making on the early modern stage

The ephemerality, mystery even, of sound in a pre-sound-recording world likely gave it an added appeal for early modern playwrights in the creation of their onstage environments. Wes Folkerth has argued, for instance, that 'Shakespeare created worlds with sound, worlds that in turn contain whole soundscapes within them' (2002: 7). Knowledge of sound in the early modern period has been bolstered by considerable recent scholarship, much of it inspired by Bruce Smith's magisterial *The Acoustic World of Early Modern England*. Smith's painstaking research allowed him to construct soundscapes across city, country and court of the time and to consider how they were produced by a variety of performance media. The chapter 'Within the Wooden O' specifically concerns the theatre as aural space. Here Smith asserts that theatres

> as instruments for the production and reception of sound ask to be thought about in different ways than theatres as frames for the mounting and viewing of spectacle. What were the acoustic properties of the instruments themselves? What were they made of? What kinds of sounds could they produce? What constituted the repertory of sounds on which playwrights and actors could draw? What qualities of the human voice figured in this repertory? (1999: 207)

Important questions all and they remind us of many of the propositions that Vitruvius tried to elucidate in his account of the construction of Greek and Roman theatres. By way of a detailed analysis of the wood, plaster and lath fabrication of the Globe Theatre, Smith notes that all these materials 'return to the ambient air a high percentage of the sound waves that strike them' (1999: 209) – excellent conditions, in fact, for projection of the male voice. He continues: 'The standing waves that create harmonically rich, in-filling sound are produced by reflections off many surfaces. In general, the more surfaces there are, the fuller the acoustic effect. As a twenty-side polygon, the Globe provided plenty of reflective surfaces' (1999: 211). An indoor and rectangular theatre (such as the Blackfriars) produced, Smith suggests, 'a "round" sound [reverberating around the theatre space] quite different from the "broad" sound of the

Globe – just the reverse of the effect suggested by the physical shapes of the two structures' (1999: 217).

Smith also conducted a comprehensive study of the 'aural contrast' between boys' and men's voices, measuring pitch and timbre to conclude: 'speech sounds gendered as male would pervade the wooden O, filling it from side to side; speech sounds gendered as female would be heard as isolated effects within this male matrix' (1999: 229). Similarly, Gina Bloom has explored what she calls 'the material attributes of the voice' (2007: 3), arguing that for 'early modern men, controlling voice – their own as well as those of subordinates (children, servants, and women) – often functioned as a signifier of manly identity' (2007: 8–9). We might extend Bloom's focus, then, to think about other sounds employed in the theatre to assert (or contradict) normative gender roles and, more generally, to examine how theatre sounds interact with stage voices to shape an audience's understanding of a play.

What, then, were the conventional theatre sounds of the period? Some evidence is available from the one extant picture of an open-air public theatre in Shakespeare's time, a sketch of The Swan made by Arnoldus Buchelius following a drawing by his friend Johannes De Witt who had visited London in 1596. This image represents the experience of theatre through four performance signifiers, two of them precisely sonic: the flag atop the thatched roof, a trumpeter in a box just below, the musicians in the gallery and actors on the stage. Theatres raised their flags to indicate the day of a performance, encouraging potential patrons to cross the river to Bankside, but a more specific alert came from the in-house trumpeter. As Tiffany Stern has noted, it is conventional in our contemporary theatres for audiences to receive visual prompts that mark the start of performance, 'the lights in the auditorium will be lowered; the lights on the stage will be raised; a stage curtain, if there is one, will part' (2015: 359). She continues:

> In the early modern period, however, the signal that told spectators to stop talking and look to the stage

was primarily aural. A trumpeter, or sometimes several trumpeters, 'heralded' the start of a play with two or three sharp blasts – or even, sometimes, an entire 'flourish' (fanfare) – on his, or their, instrument(s). (2015: 359)

As she further explains, the early modern theatregoer would be accustomed to the sound of a trumpet as a signal 'that something momentous and authoritative was about to happen', given its use in a myriad of other occasions such as proclamations, coronations and challenges (2015: 359).

The trumpet blast was often only the first of multiple sonic cues designed to grab an audience's attention. In this regard, Smith points out that 'all but a handful of Shakespeare's scripts display quite obvious devices for establishing the auditory field of the play within the first few moments' (1999: 276). It seems likely, too, that the nature of the sonic intervention might also signal to the audience the genre of the play so that they might attune their expectations accordingly. The histories and tragedies generally start with the sounds of authority: trumpets and hautboys (oboes) for *2 Henry 6*, drummers leading a march of soldiers in *3 Henry 6*, a drummer leading 'colours' for the entrance of Bassianus in *Titus Andronicus*, two fanfares to herald the entrance of King Lear, a 'flourish' for the entrance of Anthony and Cleopatra. By contrast, comedies rarely start with sound although an exception is found in Orsino's famous opening line to his musicians in *Twelfth Night*, 'If music be the food of love, play on' (1.1.1). Tragedies often deploy ominous or threatening sound in their first moments: it is a sound that provokes Barnado to cry out 'Who's there?' at the start of *Hamlet*, while *Macbeth* uses the sound of thunder to accompany the appearance of the witches. Midway through *Othello*'s opening scene, Iago and Roderigo beat on Brabantio's door and shout loudly and aggressively to wake up Desdemona's father to the news of her elopement with the Moor. An audit of extant plays from Shakespeare's time produces a substantial collection of military fanfares, trumpet blasts and drum marches yet, as David Linley stresses, these sounds 'cannot, for a modern audience, convey the precision of meaning that might have been available to an audience for whom the language of military drums and trumpets was familiar' (2008: 95). In other words, important information about characters, events and fates would have been telegraphed to the early modern audience through a familiar and shared repertory of sound.

Performances were also regularly punctuated with other kinds of sound effects, what Bruce Smith has called 'sonic scene-setting' (2013: 184). Among these were a variety of musical instruments and other apparatuses that would orchestrate the play beyond the human voice. A bell 'stood in for two objects: the public bell that stated alarm or ceremony; and the clock bell that stated time' (Stern 2013: 29). Horns were sounded to indicate a hunting party: for example, in the stage direction 'Wind horns. Enter a Lord from hunting, with his train' at the beginning of *The Taming of the Shrew* when Christopher Sly has fallen asleep only ten lines into the performance. Storms are frequent in the plays of Shakespeare and his contemporaries and while lightning is obviously visual (created, rather dangerously, with fireworks), thunder must be delivered aurally. This might have been realized through intense drumming but more usually by rolling around a cannonball in the tiring house (appropriately, then, the sound emanating from the upper level of the theatre that functioned symbolically as the heavens). Gwilym Jones has described an even more sophisticated technology, the 'thunder run': 'A wooden trough, either on a fulcrum or sloping along the floor, contains a cannonball which, when see-sawed or released, rolls. Different levels may be built into the trough, to enable separate thunderclaps to be sounded when the ball drops' (2013: 36–7). As Jones notes, *Julius Caesar* is the first of Shakespeare's plays to exploit a storm scene – a fact that coincides with the opening of the Globe (1599) and may well have been intended to promote the superior and spectacular technological capabilities of the new theatre. A 2016 archaeological excavation of the possible site of the Curtain theatre in Shoreditch, one of London's earliest public theatres (1577), uncovered a fragment of a ceramic bird whistle – a find that prompted the claim that it might well have been used in Shakespeare's *Romeo and Juliet*, a play almost certainly staged at the Curtain and replete with numerous references to bird song (MOLA 2016).

Most commonly deployed in the early modern theatre's repertoire of sound effects was, of course, music. This is hardly surprising given the penetration of music into so many aspects of early modern life. David Linley describes music in the parish churches as well as in 'communal celebration, at weddings, feasts, or church ales' where minstrels would almost always be present (2016: 135). And, as Linley puts it, the 'largest and most prestigious musical establishment was that of the royal court' (2016: 136). Actors were often also trained musicians and different theatres, to meet the size of the house, indoors or out, had different sound capabilities and different play repertoires. Some plays relied on mood music at key dramatic moments: in *The Merchant of Venice*, each of Portia's suitors enters and exits to a 'flourish of cornets' with the key stage direction '*Here music. A song the whilst BASSANIO comments on the caskets to himself*' (3.2.62). The song 'Tell me where is fancy bred' is led by 'one from Portia's train' with a refrain from 'All' that likely drew the audience into singing as well. When Richard III marshals his troops to counteract Richmond's insurgency (4.4) – '*Enter KING RICHARD and his train marching with drummers and trumpeters*' – the sound is surely intended to be intense, to summon fear and foreboding as war becomes imminent. The intimate conversation between Hamlet and Horatio ahead of the performance of 'The Murder of Gonzago' is interrupted by the entrance of the royal party indicated first as '*Enter trumpets and kettle drums. Sound a flourish*' (3.2.82) and, two lines later, '*Danish march. Enter King, Queen, Polonius, Ophelia, Rosencrantz, Guildenstern, and other lords attendant, with guard carrying torches*' (3.2.84). Here the sounds of power underscore Hamlet's distance, physically and politically, from the royal party.

Shakespeare often relies on sound to create environment as well as mood, with *As You Like It* one of his most sonically rich dramas. If the first scenes of that play conjure the violent world of the court (for example, the noisy wrestling match between Orlando and Charles), Act 2 relies on music to transport characters and audience alike to the Forest of Arden. In 2.5, Amiens and Jacques sing 'Under the Greenwood Tree', its words about harsh weather (a thematic repeated in Amiens's next song [2.7] 'Blow, blow, thou winter wind') undermining the idea of lyric pastoral that would conventionally attach to a rural setting. And, in *As You Like It*'s final act, songs prepare the stage for the marriages expected in the resolution of comic dramas. In 5.3, Pages sing 'It was lover and his lass', a popular song that survives today through its setting for voice with lute accompaniment published in Thomas Morley's *First Book of Airs* (1600); in the following scene (5.4), preparation for Rosalind and Celia's return to their appropriate gender and class roles comes in the form of a stage masque, introduced by 'Still music' (line 96) and the song 'Wedding is great Juno's crown'. Commissions of new settings or arrangements for the play's songs in more recent productions underscore how important sound remains to interpretation and contextualization: in 2011, the Barenaked Ladies were asked by the Stratford Festival (Ontario) to arrange the songs for that season's *As You Like It* (the band also released the songs as an album); in 2013, the RSC commissioned singer-songwriter Laura Marling to give their production's music a contemporary feel; and in 2016, the National Theatre in London worked with Orlando Gough, an associate artist at the Royal Opera House, for their production's unique musical arrangement.

Case study: Shakespeare's *The Tempest*

I will look here at how the playwright conjures up his stage world, the magical island setting, through an imagination of sound, as well as examines how conventions of sound typical to early modern theatrical production were deployed in the creation of the eponymous storm. We know that *The Tempest* was presented on 1 November 1611, Hallowmas Night, at Whitehall, a performance at court as part of the celebrations for Princess Elizabeth's betrothal to the Elector Palatine, and it is generally agreed that the play must have been performed earlier at one of the King's Men's venues, likely the indoor Blackfriars Theatre. As Arden editors Alden T. Vaughan and Virginia Mason Vaughan observe, the setting for the play is constant – 'one fictional island' – but the use of various sound effects is extensive and varied in the course of the action: 'thunder, confused noises, soft music, solemn music, a noise of hunters, dogs barking' (2011: 9).

The play starts with a memorable soundscape indicated in the opening stage direction – '*A tempestuous noise of thunder and lightning heard*' – sure to grab the attention of any theatre audience, then or now. Editors Vaughan and Vaughan furnish a footnote to suggest that in Shakespeare's theatre such a direction would prompt the use of a 'sea machine (pebbles in a drum)' to create the sounds of crashing waves and 'a wind machine (a loose length of canvas turned on a wheel)' for gusts of wind, drums for thunder and fireworks 'hung from a rope across the rear of the stage' for lightning (2011: 165). Not all critics agree since if *The Tempest* was, in fact, an indoor theatre play (at Blackfriars and, of course, at Whitehall), then the production was unlikely to risk fireworks, 'leaving the storm to be represented through sound alone' (Jones 2013: 39–40). Such an argument is surely supported by word choices in the relevant stage direction, 'noise' and 'heard'.

Gwilym Jones makes the important point that storms in Shakespeare's plays are never 'simply' storms: 'rather, the scenes are always concerned with human apprehension' (2013: 45). His observation reminds us that sound in theatre performance can cue a variety of responses beyond its primary representational field (here, weather). To expand Jones's comment, the sounds of the storm also set a psychological map for the play's characters: everyone will experience a personal 'tempest' in the course of the action. Moreover, throughout the play, sound orchestrates action and often underpins relationships between characters. Jones concludes: 'Even with the basic effects of a noise of thunder, Shakespeare can achieve a bewildering array of variations in what they signify' (2013: 50).

If those effects, in Scene 1, create for actors and audience alike a sense of the chaotic world on board the ship and predict a tumultuous series of events, sound (actual and cited) elsewhere in the play is fundamental to both crafting the island environment and elucidating the characters' relationship to it and to each other. Most often, Ariel is the vehicle for the play's sound. When the spirit gives Prospero an account of the action we have already witnessed in the play's opening moments, it is replete with descriptions of the sound effects that we heard: 'dreadful thunderclaps' (1.2.202) and 'the fire and cracks / Of sulphurous roaring' (1.2.203–4). Later, Ariel will become *'invisible, playing and singing'* (1.2.376) in the task to lure Ferdinand towards a meeting with Miranda. 'Come unto these yellow sands,' the first of Ariel's four songs in the play, anticipates both a lull in the storm and a couple's dance (a rehearsal, perhaps, of the choreography of Ferdinand and Miranda's courtship). A stage direction follows the main verse, '*burden dispersedly*', which suggests that Ariel is accompanied by other spirits who provide the song's chorus 'sung from various positions around the stage, or perhaps from beneath, but not in unison' (1.2.382 footnote). The words in the chorus, 'Hark, hark! Bow-wow, / The watch dogs bark, bow-wow refrain' (1.2.383–4), has led some editors and modern productions to imagine actual dogs barking – a sound effect, whether sung or not, that adds to and reveals Ferdinand's fragile and confused state. Ariel's second song, 'Full fathom five thy father lies', prompts Ferdinand to think it must be about his 'drowned father; / This is no mortal business nor no sound / That the earth owes' (1.2.406–8).

Ariel returns at key points in the action with sound, music and song labouring on behalf of Prospero's plan and no sonic intervention is more important than the third song 'While you here do snoring lie', delivered '*in Gonzalo's ear*' (2.1.300). It wakes him and then Alonso, forestalling, at the very last minute, Antonio and Sebastian's plot to kill the sleeping King of Naples. This scene is directly followed by Caliban's entrance on stage '*with a burden of wood; a noise of thunder heard*' (2.2). The sound of thunder is repeated time and again to coincide with Caliban's movements, suggesting he, like the sea in the opening scene, is part of an untamed nature that needs be regulated. In this particular scene, he meets Stephano and Trinculo whose drunkenness is indicated through discordant singing; indeed, their sonic performance serves as a stark contrast to the exquisite musical and vocal skills of Ariel that have so recently been on display. In 3.2, Ariel successfully imitates Trinculo's voice, like one of Bacon's *pantomimi*, effectively sewing dissent among the members of the newly aligned triumvirate – Stephano, Trinculo and Caliban. When Stephano tries to arrest the conflict by suggesting they sing 'Flout 'em and scout 'em, / Thought is free' (3.2.121–3), Ariel provides a musical accompaniment on tabor (drum) and pipe, unseen – terrifying the shipwrecked duo, undermining their bravado and prompting Caliban's famous (and beautiful) speech:

> Be not afeard. The isle is full of noises,
> Sounds and sweet airs that give delight and hurt not.
> Sometimes a thousand twangling instruments
> Will hum about mine ears; and sometimes voices,
> That if I then had waked after long sleep,
> Will make me sleep again; (3.2.135–40)

In both of these examples, the ear plays an important part: Ariel sings to the sleeping Gonzalo in order to save Alonso from murder, Caliban has learned to listen the island's strange soundscape for its 'delight' (what, perhaps, makes it feel like home to him). As well, Prospero initiates his revelation of the familial backstory with an imperative to Miranda to listen, 'The very minute bids thee ope thine ear' (1.2.37). In this context, Gina Bloom offers an illustration from Giogrio Barberio Corsetti's production *La Tempesta* (staged at Teatro Argentina, 2000) in which 'Miranda listens to Prospero's lecture from one of the seats in the theater auditorium. Miranda's ears become the ears of the audience, and Prospero's repeated anxieties about being heard by his daughter are linked to the actor's (and perhaps the playwright's) concerns about the wandering interests of playgoers' (2007: 155).

Miranda, of course, offers her own lecture to Caliban where the crux of her argument turns on his entry into (English) language:

> I pitied thee,
> Took pains to make thee speak, taught thee each hour
> One thing or other. When thou didst not, savage,
> Know thine own meaning, but wouldst gabble like
> A thing most brutish, I endowed thy purposes
> With words that made them known. (1.2.352–8)

The 'natural' Caliban is not accorded language by his Milanese masters but instead described as capable only of 'gabble' – one of the play's starkest moments of dehumanization and an explicit illustration of how colonial regimes imposed the English language as one particularly effective mode of discipline. Without her language lessons, Caliban, she imagines, could not understand himself or his world. Thus she shares with European colonizers 'the belief that the Indians [of the New World] had no language at all', a supposition that Stephen Greenblatt describes as '[a]rrogant, blindly obstinate, and destructive' (1990: 26). Caliban's retort is, of course, much quoted: 'You taught me language, and my profit on't / Is I know how to curse' (1.2.364–5). At the same time, Prospero's punishments – levied at Caliban's tardiness in bringing them fuel – aim to reduce the unwilling servant once again to nothing more than sound, to a state of pain beyond language:

If though neglect'st, or dost unwillingly
What I command, I'll rack thee with hold cramps,
Fill all thy bones with aches, make thee roar,
That beasts shall tremble at thy din. (1.2.369–72)

Later in the play, Prospero activates a similar strategy of torture to quell the hapless insurrection of Stephano and Trinculo: '*A noise of hunters heard. Enter diverse Spirits in shape of dogs and hounds, hunting them* [Stephano, Trinculo, Caliban] *about. Prospero and Ariel setting them on*' (4.1.254), inviting the dogs to 'grind their joints / With dry convulsions, shorten up their sinews / With aged cramps' (4.1.258–9), a reprise of the kinds of torture that earlier (1.2) threatened to render Caliban outside language.

In the second half of *The Tempest*, sound is more often produced in service of resolution and concord, preparations for the parties to return to Naples and their proper roles. Prospero lays the groundwork for his reveal to Alonso and his party first by conjuring 'Solemn and strange music' and a lavish banquet to astonish his guests (3.3). Notably, Alonso and Gonzalo react in sonic terms:

ALONSO
What harmony is this? My good friends, hark!

GONZALO
Marvellous sweet music! (3.3.18–19)

This shift in tone is, however, modified when Ariel appears to deliver a lesson to the 'three men of sin' (3.3.53) and is accompanied by thunder and lightning, recalling both the play's opening sequence and the unruliness of Caliban elsewhere in the play. The thirty-line speech demanding Alonso and his group repent concludes again with sonic cues: '*He* [Ariel] *vanishes in thunder. Then, to soft music, enter the shapes again and dance with mocks and mows, and carry out the table*' (3.3.82). This acoustic shift from harsh sounds (thunder, barking, hunters' horns) typical in the first parts of the play to 'soft music' here marks a pivotal turn in the action. Orchestrated by Prospero, events will now unfold towards harmonious settlement, at least for everyone but Caliban. The masque in 4.1 repeats the underscore of 'soft music' (stage direction at line 58) and continues with the songs and dances of the nuptial-inflected masque that Prospero has evoked. The classical sophistication and concert of the masque performance is, however, brought to an abrupt end when Prospero hears '*a strange hollow and confused noise*' (4.1.138 SD) that reminds the magus of 'the beast Caliban and his confederates' and the planned revolt. Eventually the insurgent group is despatched by a reprise of a '*noise of hunters*' and the Spirits '*in shape of dogs and hounds*' (4.1.255).

By contrast, the play's final act is almost without sound effects – only Ariel's song 'Where the bee sucks, there suck I' interrupts a focused process of resolution. This is a song that not only celebrates Ariel's approaching freedom but also accompanies Prospero's conversion visually through costume, from magician to Duke of Milan. With harmony restored between the characters, sound – and especially music – seems to have served its purpose in the play.

What this case study illustrates, then, is the interpretive framework that sound provides for the play. Whether as critical reader or performance director, audience member or stage actor, how *The Tempest* works and what it means relies on a comprehension and interpretation of its sonic register. Even in more radical adaptations – for example, Julie Taymor's film version with Helen Mirren in the role of Prospera – music remains at the heart of the play's performance. Taymor, after all, commissioned frequent collaborator Elliot Goldenthal to prepare an original soundtrack and Goldenthal not only reworked the songs of Shakespeare's text but also added others ('Alchemical Lightshow', 'Brave New World' and 'Lava Dogs', among them). Goldenthal's twelve songs for Taymor's film were also released as an album. A. O. Scott, reviewing the film for the *New York Times*, described Taymor's interpretation 'a visual stew' accompanied by a 'musical sauce, full of lumps and clashing flavors' (2010) – a caution, perhaps, to the consequences of a poorly integrated sonic environment.

The Tempest was, moreover, one of the most performed plays of the Restoration period. The John Dryden–William Davenant adaptation, which premiered in 1667, 'constituted a tenth of all live performances on both stages in its first season' (Shanahan 2013: 91) and was praised by Samuel Pepys, among others, for its 'echo' music. In 1673–4, Thomas Shadwell adapted the Dryden–Davenant version as an opera, using music by five different composers and, as Julie Muller notes, most of the characters are sung *for* in this reworking of the play (1994: 192). The opening stage direction indicates a 'Band of 24 Violins, with the Harpsicals and Theorbo's [large bass lute]' to accompany the sounds of thunder and lightning conventional to the production of the storm (Vaughan and Vaughan 2011: 79). While this version was by far the most popular of the eighteenth century, David Garrick produced his own opera *Tempest* in 1756 where '[t]he text was cut to make room for thirty-two songs' (Vaughan and Vaughan 2011: 83). Charles Kean's 1857 version – some five hours long, even as the text was drastically cut – opened with 'an immensely realistic shipwreck scene … in which the dialogue was inaudible' (Booth 1981: 49). Indeed, for almost two hundred years, *The Tempest* was primarily a spectacular musical rather than Shakespeare's play – an extended sonic interlude, then, in the drama's extensive history of production and adaptation.

A sonic imagination of early modern London

Notwithstanding my earlier scepticism about claims for original practices, authentic performance methodologies suggest another route through which we might approach the sounds of historically remote drama. Jonathan Sterne argues that studying the past requires 'sonic imaginations' that are 'plural, recursive, reflexive, driven to represent, refigure and redescribe' (2012: 5). For Sterne, these 'imaginations' are built on relationships between different sonic phenomena 'whether they be music, voices, listening, media, buildings, performances or another other path into sonic life' (2012: 3). Similarly, Bruce Smith asks: 'What kinds of sounds did Shakespeare and his contemporaries hear? What kinds of sounds occurred in the world around them? What kinds of sounds did they make themselves?' (2004: 22)

To apply these ideas to the theatres of ancient Greece or Shakespeare's London requires movement beyond the isolation of particular elements (voice, music, sound effects) and, more generally, the theatre setting towards a more thorough mapping of what Sterne so usefully calls an event's 'sonic life'. How can we approach the sound archive of a more extended geography in which a performance once took place? This suggests that we need to consider, like Vitruvius, the properties of the sites where theatre was staged.

A productive model can be found in Maarten Walraven's 'History and Its Acoustic Context: Silence, Resonance, Echo and Where to Find Them in the Archive', an essay that asks the listening historian to work beyond and outside the 'earwitnesses of aural culture' to understand sound both as an object of study and as the acoustic context of an event. His approach suggests that we investigate not just the impact of the physical properties of the playing space but also locate them – and the ways those places were heard – in the sound culture of the period. Walraven asserts that the study of sound must encompass qualities like noise and silence alongside music and voice; indeed, he suggests that the acoustic environment of a neighbourhood will produce and determine the experience of a particular sound in a particular place. To grasp the power and meaning of such a sound in such a place, Walraven proposes that researchers extend discussion of aural architecture to include the neighbourhood contextual to a sound's production. This might include, for the performance of a Shakespeare play, the other buildings immediately contiguous and in the streets around the theatre, the surfaces that performers and audiences travel to reach that theatre (the street, the river) and the sounds of human bodies themselves as components in the formation of a specific environment as well as in its passers-by. Historically informed performance, then, would try to capture a Globe Theatre sound event in the full scope of its technical conditions within the playing space and beyond, as part of a map that composed a sound profile of the Southwark area and the River Thames. Productions at today's Shakespeare's Globe, a replica theatre on more or less the same site as its predecessors, can signal this kind of aural archaeology so that it might inform our 'sonic imaginations'. For instance, David Crystal refers to a twenty-first-century production of *The Tempest* at the Globe and describes a moment when Caliban delivered his 'This isle is full of noises' speech (3.2) 'and to everyone's delight, a pair of river-boats hooted' (2005: 7). This is not just a sound-based 'bonus' to the pleasure of the text realized serendipitously for a modern audience but an active sonic trace of the history of a river that was the primary travel corridor and economic engine of early modern London.

A sonic methodology, Walraven suggests, must seek 'to re-compose the interplay of humans and their environment through sound' and, in this way, 'historians must pay attention to the resonances, both psychical and physical, within that environment. In doing so, historians can understand how people used the resonances in their environments, urban or rural, home or public, to create communities' (2013). To re-compose the soundscape of the Globe of Shakespeare's time, a historian might turn, among other things, to period documents (maps, laws, images, playtexts) about neighbourhoods and thoroughfares in early modern London so as to discover traces of sound. For example, we might examine complaints about an excess of urban noise or records of exceptional events of celebration or disturbance. Smith, in his discussion of the 'acoustic archaeologist', notes of London that 'church bells still hang in some of the same belfries and can still be rung. Some of the same interior spaces still exist, and their acoustic properties can still be experienced' (2004: 22). Such sources might add to our knowledge of the normative interpretive frameworks that players and audiences might apply to the sounds produced and heard in the theatre. At stake, Walraven argues, is 'the audibility of history' (2013).

Any reading or production of a play from ancient Greece or England's early modern period can only benefit from a more comprehensive knowledge of what I've called here 'classical sound'. A sonic approach makes available new strategies of comprehension and/or of direction and design as the incorporation of the *aulos* into The Actors Theatre Company production of *The Suppliant Women* so powerfully demonstrated: a very contemporary adaptation (to address the perils experienced by migrant populations in the twenty-first century) utilized the ancient soundtrack to access for its audiences a millennia-long history of the dangers faced by refugees. As well, to focus on sound is to open up new research topics on the theatres of these historical pasts even if, as Barthes wrote of Greek theatre, 'our archaeology affords us incomplete information' (1985: 87).

The nineteenth century is, of course, much more commonly described as having ushered in a 'pictoral culture, and the theatre was also pictoral' (Booth 1991: 95). As Michael Booth described it: 'Looking at the world through the medium of pictures ... became a habit in the first half of the nineteenth century, and as the pictorial means of information grew more sophisticated and better adapted to mass public consumption, the bombardment of visual and specifically pictorial stimuli became inescapable' (1981: 8). The stage, framed now by the proscenium arch, borrowed from the visual displays in shop windows and the scenes portrayed in dioramas. The theatre created its most spectacular effects from new advances in lighting technology with sound and music relegated to little more than a backdrop to a visually compelling scene. In Booth's words: 'To look at the stage as if it were a picture was by 1859 an automatic response in audiences, and to make performance resemble painting was a habit of managers and technical staff' (1981: 10). Such a focus on the stage as a visually realized art 'rendered sound a secondary epistemic object' (Dyson 2013: 419). Indeed, the drawing-room dramas that predominated mainstream stages from the advent of realism until at least the mid-twentieth century were much more prosaic in their use of even the most modest sound effects: for example, the door bell that would herald the arrival of new characters into the fourth-wall-removed setting.

David Collison describes the theatres of Victorian melodrama as marking the 'final days of effects machines' (2008: 38). But, at the same time, it was also a period coincident with the rapid development of technologies for sound recording and amplification. Indeed, the first use of recorded sound in a theatrical production took place in 1890, in a performance at Terry's Theatre in London of *The Judge* (a three-act farce by Arthur Law) when audiences heard 'an offstage phonographic playing of a baby's cry' (Booth 1991: 93). From this very simple beginning, sound recording and related technologies would soon become commonplace elements of theatrical production and, indeed, constitutive elements of twentieth-century avant-garde performance.

SECTION TWO

Avant-Garde Sound

New technologies for sound performance

If mainstream theatres of the late nineteenth and early twentieth centuries were determinedly pictorial – for example, the 'act-ending tableaux' that presented 'a combination of scenery, furniture, properties and actors frozen in action just as on a canvas' (Booth 1991: 95) – emergent avant-garde art forms revelled in new and innovative possibilities for sound, particularly inspired and made available by the rapid proliferation of machine-based technologies. Rather than prolong the 'ocularcentrism' that was for so long the focus of criticism about art forms from the late nineteenth century and into the twentieth century, Adrian Curtin, in his ground-breaking book *Avant-Garde Theatre Sound*, insists that 'modernity was crucially informed by sonic phenomena' (2014: 8).

Curtin explains that a burgeoning aesthetic interest in sound during this period was produced by way of a whole host of environmental changes, as well as in recognition of the potentials offered in the appropriation of those newly invented machines for artistic production. Among the most significant influences, he includes 'increased noise levels and dense sonic environments of modern metropolises', 'being able to preserve the sound of one's own voice and the voices of others using sound-recording technology' and 'conceiving of sound as a "thing"-like entity that can be purchased and owned (e.g. a gramophone recording)' (2014: 9–10). In other words, and not surprisingly, experimental theatre makers were not only thoroughly engaged with how technological inventiveness might expand the possibilities of sound for their own performances of modernity but how they might harvest the sounds of everyday urban life as art. That sound is such a key feature of the Modern period is, too, evidenced by the first appearance of the word 'sonic' in the *Oxford English Dictionary*. The dictionary cites the May 1923 issue of *Scientific American* for its example of the word's inaugural use: 'Sonic sounding is rendered possible by the fact that sound vibrations, passing through water and striking a solid surface, are returned as an echo to the source from which they originated.' But, by 1923, explorations of the sonic had already become vital to both theories and practices of avant-garde performance.

On 20 February 1909, 'The Founding and Manifesto of Futurism' by Filippo Tomaso Marinetti appeared as an advertisement on the front page of the Paris newspaper *Le Figaro*. In its one-and-a-half columns, Marinetti's document declared the advent of the Futurist movement 'because we want to free this land [Italy] from its smelly gangrene of professors, archaeologists, ciceroni [tour guides], and antiquarians' (1972: 42) and set out eleven principles as a manifesto. The last of these principles reads:

> We will sing of great crowds excited by work, by pleasure, and by riot; we will sing of the multicolored, polyphonic tides of revolution in the modern capitals; we will sing of the vibrant nightly fervor of arsenals and shipyards blazing with violent electric moons; greedy railway stations that devour smoke – plumed serpents; factories hung on clouds by the crooked lines of their smoke; bridges that stride the rivers like giant gymnasts, flashing in the sun with a glitter

of knives; adventurous steamers that sniff the horizon; deep-chested locomotives whose wheels paw the tracks like the hooves of enormous steel horses bridled by tubing; and the sleek flight of planes whose propellers chatter in the wind like banners and seem to cheer like an enthusiastic crowd. (1972: 42)

Marinetti captured, for the Futurists and their potential audiences, what he felt was the stultifying presence of history and the exhilarating possibilities of the new: transportation and industry, the sounds and sights and smells of the urban environment which promised 'the habit of energy and fearlessness' in the world to come (1972: 41).

Some six years later, Marinetti, with Emilio Settimelli and Bruno Corr, elaborated on the 1909 salvo with their co-authored publication of 'The Futurist Synthetic Theatre' (18 February 1915). This was a declaration that sought action to replace the structures of traditional theatre since it was 'too prolix, analytic, pedantically psychological, explanatory, diluted, finicking, static, as full of prohibitions as a police station, as cut up into cells as a monastery, as moss-grown as an old abandoned house' (1972: 123–4). Synthetic theatre would instead be only brief in its duration and 'destroy the technique ... from the Greeks until now' (1972: 125). Among the many plays of Italian Futurism, Francesco Cangiulio's drama '*Detonazione*' (*Detonation*) provides an exemplary illustration of both the sparseness of the performance and the starkness of a sonic response to experiences of war. Both the manifesto and the play itself were written in 1915, the second year of the First World War. Cangiulio's play, in its entirety, reads:

SYNTHESIS OF ALL MODERN THEATRE
CHARACTER
A BULLET
Road at night, cold, deserted.
A minute of silence. – A gunshot.
CURTAIN   (1970: 131)

Marinetti himself wrote in a variety of genres but garnered most attention for his sound poems or words-in-freedom, as he described them in the 'Destruction of Syntax – Radio Imagination – Words-in-Freedom' (11 May 1913); the sound-poet, Marinetti wrote, 'will begin by brutally destroying the syntax of his speech. He will not waste time in constructing periodic sentences. He could care less about punctuation or finding the right adjective' (Rainey 2009: 149). In the place of traditional poetics, he proposed that the sound-poet 'will assault your nerves with visual, auditory, olfactory sensations, just as their insistent pressure in him demands. The rush of steam-emotion will burst the steampipe of the sentence, the valves of punctuation, and the regular clamp of the adjective. Fistfuls of basic words without any conventional order' (Rainey 2009: 149). To achieve these goals, Marinetti described a typographical revolution that would be required by the sound-poem, but, as Curtin reminds us, Marinetti was not only looking to realize his sound-poems in a radically new print layout. He also performed this material. In April 1919, Marinetti staged *Zong Toomb Toomb* in London, a work inspired by his time as a war reporter at the 1912–13 Battle of Adrianople and described by Claire Warden as a sound-poem that 'morphs into a war report' through its performance (2015: 123). The live-action version of *Zong Toomb Toomb* was, to be sure, replete with sound: Marinetti's work required the 'use of a telephone, some boards, and "the right sort of hammers" to act out the orders of the Turkish general and simulate artillery fire; off-stage drums (played on cue in another room)' (Curtin 2014: 168). Wyndham Lewis, in the London audience, claimed that 'even at the front, when bullets whistled around him, he had never encountered such a terrifying volume of noise as Marinetti produced' (Thompson 2002: 143).

'The Futurist Synthetic Theatre' was undoubtedly the most influential of the many manifestos, 'programmatic for the acoustic turn in the arts and theatre of the twentieth and twenty-first centuries' (Ovadija 2016: 27). Indeed, the Italian Futurists insisted that the realities of a Modern soundscape – and particularly as it had been shaped and experienced in the context of the First World War – required 'a poetics open to the forces exerted by the new technologies of transportation, communication and information' (Kahn 2013: 95). This poetics demanded, as Curtin illustrates, a refusal of the passive and silent behaviour of audience members in traditional theatres: the Futurists, he notes, 'established noise as a principal component of the *serate*, theatrical evenings ... riling spectators into actively participating in the performance by disrupting it in some fashion' (2014: 154). What Futurist performance encouraged was, in effect, an experiential and interactive theatre, a genre that has again become popular and pervasive in early twenty-first-century forms, although descriptions of audience participation in the *serate* make the carefully controlled environments of productions such as Punchdrunk's *Sleep No More* seem rather tame and pedestrian:

> Typically, audiences [at a *serata*] did not just holler, boo, laugh, and whistle at Marineti and his fellow futurists, but threw vegetables and other missiles at them (bought especially for the occasion), set off firecrackers, honked horns, blew on whistles and pipes, struck cow-bells, and got into fights with the performers and with each other, giving rise to a violent, carnivalesque affair. (Curtin 2014: 154)

Case study: Luigi Russolo's intonarumori and 'The Art of Noise'

Given the raucous soundscapes of the *serate*, both onstage and offstage, it is no surprise that among the many Futurist publications one was dedicated to a theorization of 'The Art of Noise' (Luigi Russolo's manifesto of 1913). Its author was chiefly a painter and a composer, but this work is important to theatre sound both for Russolo's elaboration of the aesthetic properties of noise and for his invention of a range of twenty-seven noise machines called intonarumori (which he assembled as an 'orchestra'). These intonarumori were designed specifically to put Russolo's own theories into practice. Simply described, the instruments were sound boxes with a large speaker mounted on the front side and operated by the musician via a hand crank:

> The cranked wheel would rub a string attached to a single diaphragm, stretched on a cylindrical resonator sending sound out through the funnel [speaker]. This created a wide array of sounds, which could be tuned and rhythmically regulated by means of mechanical manipulation. The pitch was regulated by a lever on top of the box that continually increased or reduced the tension and length of a vibrating string, allowing for an infinite number of musical intervals divided into semitones, quartertones, and smaller fractions of the eharmonic scale. Different rhythms and timbres were obtained by the physical or chemical preparation of parts of the instrument. (Ovadija 2016: 124–5)

Russolo's manifesto, written in the form of a letter to Balilla Pratella (who had himself written manifestos on Futurist music), starts in the same vein as Marinetti's 1909 document – an attack on the classical: 'The Greeks ... have limited the domain of music until now and made almost impossible the harmony they were unaware of' (Russolo 2013: 75). And, as in Marinetti's work, it is modern life that has prompted a 'revolution' away from 'musical art' to '**noise-sound**': 'In the pounding atmosphere of great cities as well as in the formerly silent countryside, machines create today such a large number of varied noises that pure sound, with its littleness and its monotony, now fails to arouse any emotion' (2013: 76, bolding in original). Russolo argues that the noise-sound of transportation and massed crowds in a city produce more pleasure than listening to a symphony – to be specific, Russolo pejoratively calls it '**listening once more**' to the exhaustingly familiar sounds of symphonic compositions (2013: 76, bolding in original).

What Russolo saw as radical was the opportunity both for hearing sounds that had not been heard in the world before and for demonstrating how these newly experienced realities were fundamentally affective. The impact of the sonic environment on the theories expounded by the Futurists cannot be underestimated and, indeed, their work may well represent the pivot between classical sound production in the theatre and the multiplicity of sound economies in theatres and other performance spaces that have developed in the Modern period and since. Bruce Smith, whose work on the soundscapes of Shakespeare's theatre was discussed in Section One, acknowledges the decisiveness of this paradigm shift: 'Two inventions – electricity and the internal combustion engine – make it difficult for us even to imagine what life in early modern England would have sounded like' (1999: 39). In other words, technological developments in the Modern age have inevitably constricted research about sound in historical periods before then. The post-nineteenth-century human ear can never actually experience what it was to hear before industrialization.

Russolo's manifesto, however, was focused on the creativity, inspiration and excitement that a new world of sound might offer to artists early in the twentieth century. He urges an acoustic consciousness to meet the demands of urban life:

> Let's walk together through a great modern capital, with the ear more attentive than the eye, and we will vary the pleasures of our sensibilities by distinguishing among the gurglings of water, air and gas inside metallic pipes, the rumbling and rattling of engines breathing with obvious animal spirits, the rising and falling of pistons, the stridency of mechanical saws, the loud jumping of trolleys on their rails, the snapping of whips, the whipping of flags. We will have fun imagining our orchestration of department stores' sliding doors, the hubbub of the crowds, the different roars of railroad stations, iron foundries, textile mills, printing houses, power plants and subways. (2013: 77)

Strikingly, his imperative for a city encountered and comprehended by a sonic *flâneur* anticipates Walter Benjamin's more visual-spatial urban walker in the arcades of Paris by almost two decades. In fact, Benjamin, far from embracing the thrills Russolo found in a deluge of urban sound, wrote grumpily of its constraints on typical human interaction: 'With the steady increase in traffic on the streets, it was only the macademization [ashphalt laid over the cobblestones] of the roadways that made it possible in the end to have a conversation on the terrace of a café without shouting in the other person's ear' (1999: 420, M2,5 in 'Convolutes').

If Benjamin wanted to retain the quieter pleasures of bourgeois café culture, Russolo, by contrast, was a champion of human shouting. Indeed, it was a component of one of the six 'categories' of noise that he suggested Futurism should generate through new technologies of performance. He did not assign these six categories identifying titles but simply presented cluster groups of noises without any particular rationale for the arrangement:

1	2
roars	whistles
claps	snores
noises of falling water	snorts
driving noises	
bellows	

3	4
whispers	shrill sounds
mutterings	cracks
rustlings	buzzings
grumbles	jingles
grunts	shuffles
gurgles	

5	6
percussive noises using metal, wood, skin, stone, baked earth, etc.	animal and human voices: shouts, moans, screams, laughter, rattlings, sobs

(2013: 79)

Since neither words nor traditional musical instruments were up to the task of capturing the noise-sound complexities of the Modern condition, Russolo looked to new instrumentation that might do so. It makes sense, in the context of the Futurists' dizzying appreciation of the sounds of machines, that Russolo would construct his own to manufacture a repertoire of noises that could deliver the 'special acoustic pleasure' of his art (2013: 79): these were the intonarumori. The first performance of noise-sound, enacted by the first of his intonarumori, the *scoppiatore* (which apparently emitted the sound of a spark-ignition engine across two octaves), was at a *serata* hosted by Marinetti in Milan in August 1913. Marinetti promised that the performance would give the audience 'pleasant feelings' (Maina 2011) but Russolo's *scoppiatore* were drowned out by the even noisier audience, by now accustomed to full-on vocal participation in Futurist events. A second performance in Milan the following year produced considerably more drama as Marinetti himself described:

> While the angry but imperturbable Luigi Russolo is directing precise and painstaking I go down through a side door [at the Teatro Dal Verme] and hurl myself against the first row
>
> We slap them around cramming our fists down their jeering throats and left and right Futurists and carabineers [armed soldiers] fists flying body against body egged on by Lydia [*sic*] Borelli's white clapping hands in her private box until the mad crush sends us hurtling through a trapdoor on stage down to the lowest cellar and the newspaper *Il Secolo* noted that although the Futurists were booed they didn't get the worst of the fracas since the eleven people who were

injured and brought to the hospital were all passéists. (Flint 1971: 285, missing punctuation in the original)

If the clapping of actress Borelli provided Marinetti with the rhythmic soundtrack to what seems, for him, to have been the most invigorating part of the performance – violent interactions with spectators – Russolo was unimpressed with the boisterous audience members and the carabineers who intervened: he pursued a lawsuit after the event.

Notwithstanding negative responses and violent assaults, Russolo nonetheless persevered with his intonarumori performances, staged in major European cities such as London (1914) and Paris (1921). Curtin astutely points out that, ironically, 'Russolo's preferred mode of response for his noise music ... was in the tradition of musical idealism, focused listening. This is further evident from the fact that Russolo adopted the organizational structure of symphonic music' (Curtin 2014: 160–1). At best, Russolo's noise-sound performances were artistic curiosities and his machine-instruments useful additions to the repertoire of other Futurists performers. For example, Marinetti incorporated an intonarumori orchestra into his play *Il Tamburo di Fuoco* (*The Fire Drum*) (1922), but 'the instruments were reduced to playing "background music" and providing sound effects' (Kirby and Kirby 1986: 38).

What to make of these extraordinary performances? They are not just examples of avant-garde eccentricities whose regular theatrical revival seems unlikely, even as an academic experiment, but they also mark an important turn towards sound innovation, a moment where a rejection of conventional theatre sound collided with an embrace of extra-theatrical noises. Furthermore, the theory and practices of the Italian Futurists (and of other allied artistic movements like Dada, Bruitism and Expressionism) underpin and inform later avant-garde theatrical developments such as the work of John Cage which this section will also explore. These Futurist performances are, too, the sonic ground zero for the experiential theatres of this book's third section, a connective tissue between modernity and a twenty-first-century predilection for genres such as audio walks, 'headphone' theatre and other sound-dense performance installations. They presage, too, the contemporary turn towards a more participatory theatre.

Hanging on the telephone: Sigmund Freud and Roland Barthes

The experimental performances of Marinetti and Russolo in the first decades of the twentieth century looked to create sonic worlds that would refuse traditional theatrical conventions for sound production and reception and, in their place, capture the polyphony of modern life as the matter of performance. By the 1930s, however, the first technologies of sound recording and reproduction had moved into the mainstream of society and, thus, into artistic production. The telephone and the phonograph – signature inventions of an acoustical era – would be joined by other important sound developments: the first 'talking' film (*The Jazz Singer*, 1927), the first electronically amplified record players (1926) and the first tape recorders (such as the Blattnerphone that was first used by the BBC in 1932). And these new technologies promised a wealth of performance advantages, not the least of which was as a cost-saving measure. David Collison cites 'one of the first documented examples of records used in the theatre' from an article in a 1932 volume of *Scientific American* (volume 146, January–June): it contained a report about a production of *Hamlet* in New York where 'the prelude, overture, and entire musical accompaniment to the show were reproduced over the system – there being no orchestras or other conventional music used in connection with the play' (2008: 110). This early twentieth-century example reminds us, moreover, of the ubiquity of recorded music and sound in contemporary theatre and performance. This fact alone suggests that performance analyses need to furnish more explicit recognition of the place of recorded music and sound and its relevance to the seemingly perennial interrogation of what, exactly, constitutes liveness.

But to return our focus to the contributions of new technologies to theatre and performance practice in the first half of the twentieth century, we can see that these new machines did more than put some theatre orchestras out of work: they also prompted new streams of revenue generation and, at the same time, extended the parameters of the theatrical event. The *théâtrephone* (invented by Clément Ader and given its first public demonstration in 1881) had allowed users to connect by telephone to 'the Opéra, the Opéra Comique, the Comédie-Française and the Concerts Colonne' for a few minutes at a time (Curtin 2014: 88). Launched in the 1890s, the *théâtrephone*, 'an expensive "theater chez soi" home subscription service', provided unlimited access to performances and gave subscribers the option to purchase additional sets of earphones so that group listening would be possible (Van Drie 2015: 76, 80). London had a similar service from 1895, providing live relays from theatres, churches and the Royal Opera House (Crook 1999: 17). In 1907, Lee de Forest (often described as the 'father' of American radio) proclaimed: 'It will soon be possible to distribute grand opera music from transmitters placed on the stage of the Metropolitan Opera House by a radio telephone station on the roof to almost any dwelling in Greater New York and vicinity ... The same applies to large cities. Church music, lectures, etc., can be spread abroad by the Radio Telephone' (cited in Reidy et al. 2016: 18). And, of course, the immensely popular twenty-first-century performance-to-screen transmissions (best known through the extensive worldwide availability of National Theatre's NT Live programming) had their genesis in these sound-only distributions to remote venues.

The Paris *théâtrephone* and its imitators in London, New York and elsewhere were not just curiosities, however. Rather they marked a new intermediality possible for theatre production: as Melissa Van Drie notes, 'the performance was transformed into sound and imagined in the spectator's mind. Audition is granted a creative role' (2015: 81). Put another way, sound is experienced internally by the listener who, thus, realizes the performance. The innovations in sound relay made possible by telephone technology did not only offer up new ways to reach theatre audiences but also generated new material for onstage exploration. The following case study looks at how expansion of the sound-listening dynamic exploited what Jonathan Sterne has called the 'sonic imagination'.

Case study: Jean Cocteau's *The Human Voice*

As Sterne has explained, the introduction of commercially available technologies for the distribution of sound meant that '[p]eople had to learn how to understand the relations between sounds made by people and sounds made by machines' (2003: 216). The arrival of the telephone into individual households thus provoked extended examination of the instrument's social and psychological impacts on human relationships – Sigmund Freud, for example, argued that the telephone allowed the subject to 'hear at distances which would be respected as unattainable even in a fairy tale' (1930: 4408). And it was a pervasive fascination with the telephone that lent the technological *raison d'être* for Jean Cocteau's monodrama *The Human Voice* (*La Voix Humaine*). The play was first performed at the Comédie-Française on 17 February 1930 with Berthe Bovy in the play's single role. In his 'Author's Preface' to the print edition, Cocteau describes *The Human Voice* 'as a pretext for an actress' (1951: 8) and notes, too, that he 'gave this act to the Comédie-Française in order to break with the worst prejudice: that of the young theatre groups versus the state theatres' (1951: 9). *The Human Voice* was written for an audience of traditional theatre that Cocteau thought had unfortunately remained 'a public hungry for sentiment' (1951: 9) and in the knowledge that younger, more fashionable spectators had left for 'the cinema and the so-called "avant-garde"stages' (1951: 9). Yet his play, although set in the conventional room of the fourth-wall-removed theatre, is as fascinated with the affective impacts of sound as any Futurist performance. Cocteau's text exploits what Ella Finer has described as telephonic technology's ability to 'play tricks with the distance between speaker and listener by scaling down by a false immediacy, as the electric wires mediate the distance instead of breath and air' (2017: 16).

The Human Voice opens with a dramatization of this new co-dependency between people and their sound machines: the unnamed female character is attempting to make a phone call but struggling with the complexities of shared service. Commonplace in the early days of domestic telephone use, she is using a 'party line' – a local telephone circuit that was shared by more than one user; if someone was talking on the line and another party to that line picked up, they could hear the conversation of that first user. Appropriate 'party line' etiquette (particularly, equitable sharing of line time) was not always easily resolved and the correct routing of a new call was far from guaranteed so that a successful phone connection often required the involvement of an operator at the local telephone exchange. 'Someone's calling me and I can't answer', Cocteau's character tells the operator, 'There are people on the line. Tell that woman to ring off' (1951: 21). At this point, the speaker hangs up on the call she was trying to make, only for her phone to ring at once:

> Hello, is that you, dear? … … is it you? … … Yes …. it's very difficult to hear …. you sound ever such a long way off … … Hello! … … Oh! it's awful … … there are several people on the line … … Ask them to put you through again … … Hello! *Ask them to put you through again … … … … … … … … …* I said: ask them to put you through to me again. (1951: 21–2)

Like Marinetti's words-in-freedom, the text for *The Human Voice* deploys typographical innovation to capture the sonic pace of a telephone conversation, using spaced ellipses to indicate silences of varied lengths: Cocteau's ellipsis use runs from the conventionally accepted three to indicate omission in a standard English sentence to as many as ninety-six! Indeed, his short play is choreographed by sound and sometimes by the lack of it, and the audience is asked to listen in (a real-life replication of the experience of using a party telephone line). The task of the woman's performance is to listen to what spectators cannot: the other end of the conversation.

The telephone enacts as 'injunction to listen' and, as Roland Barthes would later argue, it demands 'the total interpellation of one subject by another: it places above everything else the quasi-physical contact of the subjects (by voice and ear)' (1976, in Barthes 1985: 251). In *The Human Voice*, then, the audience hears one half of a conversation, that of the woman, talking with a man who has, until very recently, been her lover. As the man expects the woman to listen, so Cocteau requires the audience to listen to her, a sounding out of Barthes's act of total interpellation. In the play, it becomes clear that this is the phone call that will mark the end of the couple's relationship and it is disclosed eventually that the man is about to married to someone else. By turns, the woman is suicidal, hopeful, grateful, distraught, desperate and loving; the man (at least insofar as her responses to him are reliable witnesses of his words – and they may not be) expresses guilt and worry about her present emotional state and future life. Curtin describes Cocteau's play as staging 'the crossover between telephony and human desire. It showcases the dark side of the telephone's ability to provide – or prohibit – pleasure' (2014: 94).

The audience for *The Human Voice* has no sonic evidence, of course, that the speaker does in fact have an interlocutor at the end of her phone line or, at least, not necessarily the one an audience might imagine for her through the words she speaks in apparent reply. *The Human Voice* also flirts with the revelation of the woman's unconscious mind, desires and drives that emerge in the one-sided stream-of-consciousness monologue that she performs – what Cocteau calls, in his preface to the text, 'all the strange, deep tones which the voice assumes in that instrument' (1951: 7). It is useful, then, to remember that Freud had, as early as 1912, taken up the metaphor of telephone conversation to explain unconscious communication as well as to describe a method for the (listening) analyst:

> To put it in a formula: he [the analyst] must turn his own unconscious like a receptive organ towards the transmitting unconscious of the patient. He must adjust himself to the patient as a telephone receiver is adjusted to the transmitting microphone. Just as the receiver converts back into sound waves the electric oscillations in the telephone line which were set up by sound waves, so the doctor's unconscious is able, from the derivatives of the unconscious which are transmitted to him, to reconstruct that unconscious, which has determined the patient's free-associations. (1912: 2470)

As the receiver (the telephone, the audience) is the analyst of the woman's crisis so the play's ending literally drops the connection. The woman has been lying on the bed, hugging the receiver close to her body and inciting the end-to-come:

> I'm brave. Be quick. Break off. Quick. Break. I love you, I love you, I love you, I love you, I love you. … … … … …

With that string of ellipses, all that remains are Cocteau's stage directions: the telephone receiver falls to the floor (in fact, the play's last sound) followed by the instruction '*Curtain*' (1951: 48).

Roland Barthes described the telephone as 'the archetypal instrument of modern listening', suggesting it

> collects the two partners into an ideal (and, under certain circumstances, an intolerable) inter-subjectivity, because this instrument has abolished all senses except that of hearing:

the order of listening which any telephonic communication inaugurates invites the Other to collect his [sic] whole body in his voice and announces that I am collecting all of myself in my ear. (1977, in Barthes 1985: 252)

Cocteau's dramatic meditation on 'the order of listening' has proven popular in theatre repertoire, even as telephone apparatuses and networks have become ever more sophisticated and other archetypal instruments in our listening economies have come into quotidian use. For example, the Toneelgroep Amsterdam production of *The Human Voice* (2008), directed by Ivo van Hove, adopted the cordless phone so that actor Halina Reijn could pace back and forth in her tiny apartment while talking. As well, in this version, one of Cocteau's carefully crafted and ellipses-scored silences was replaced by a burst of music from the woman's MP3 player. Yet, surprisingly perhaps, van Hove's more contemporary interpretation chose to privilege space as much as, if not more than, the play's soundscape. The synopsis on the Toneelgroep Amsterdam website reads: 'It feels as if she is imprisoned in her own apartment, and at times she roams her limited space like a caged animal' – a concept realized by Jan Versweyveld's claustrophobic set design.

Versweyveld trapped Reijn's character in a minimalist glass box with a sliding glass door, suggesting a balcony high above street level and serving as the only visible exit from the oppressive situation; in other words, her constraints were spatial, casting the audience as voyeurs at least as much as eavesdroppers. Is it inevitable that twenty-first-century interpretations default to a visual economy? Or does this kind of revival of a Modernist aesthetic, through its use of sound, instead challenge the sway of an ocular-centric theatre? I think that van Hove's adaptation of *The Human Voice* for contemporary audiences was not only concerned with a kind of visual incarceration but also purposively sonic in its incorporation of 'jarring sound effects and a doom-laden musical score' (Morrow 2011). Like the minimalist environments of the Italian Futurists a century earlier, Versweyveld's design embraced the sounds and noise of an urban landscape: the actor was required at one point to slide open the door (which she could not move through – there was no stage space beyond it) and hear the energy of a world from which she is estranged and in which, it is implied, her about-to-be-former lover is at liberty. While both Freud and Barthes saw the telephone as a metaphor for unspoken human desire, where 'the listener's silence will be as active as the locutor's speech' (1977, in Barthes 1985: 252), van Hove and Versweyveld's collaboration leveraged updated sound technology and the ubiquity of its use in the everyday to make the same point: 'While waiting for her ex to call back, she listens on her iPod – not without poignancy – to Beyoncé's *Single Ladies (Put a Ring on It)*' (Morrow 2011).

For Barthes, 'there is no human voice which is not an object of desire – or of repulsion …. Every relation to a voice is necessarily erotic' (1985: 280) and in Cocteau's *The Human Voice*, acts of speaking and listening (and eavesdropping) cohere as a shared fantasy, an erotic performance mediated for all parties by the sonic capacity of the telephone. We will return to the sensory stimulation of this particular technology in Section Three by examining Janet Cardiff's audio-video walk 'The Telephone Call' (2001).

The sounds of silence: John Cage's future of music

While avant-garde performances in the first half of the twentieth century had been driven by a celebratory embrace of both new technologies and the cacophony of sounds that dominated modern city living, by the 1950s this enthusiasm had been exhausted and even overturned. This was not the result of the degradations in day-to-day living that urban congestion produced nor even a burgeoning sense of the sonic and other contamination that industrialization and concomitant mechanization had caused to the environment. Rather it was an inevitable outcome of the experiences of two world wars. Yet the appalling losses of human life that new technologies of war had caused – and the traumatic stress of wartime living (often felt at its most terrifying via sound: the air-raid siren, the strange buzzing noise of the V1 'doodlebug' bombs that showered London in 1944) – hardly slowed the exploration, and theorization, of sonic performances. It was just that everyone had become a lot less enthusiastic about noise. This section takes as its primary example one of the best-known works of this post-war period, John Cage's '4'33"', a composition that is often referred to (wrongly) as silent. In both his theoretical writings and performance compositions, Cage shifted the acoustical context for sound production, to take account of new environments in which he wanted sound to be heard and understood.

The first recital of '4'33"' took place on 29 August 1952 when pianist David Tudor came on stage inside the tiny Maverick Concert Hall in Woodstock, New York, to play two works by Cage. The first of these, a composition that had previously debuted in New York City, was called 'Water Music' (the title of an ironic replication, no doubt, of the much-beloved baroque classic composed by George Frideric Handel). Often considered to be Cage's first performance piece, the six-minute 'Water Music' is replete with a variety of sounds including some generated by the use of a radio, several different bird-whistles, a deck of cards and containers of water. The score indicates that the pianist will realize forty-one different sound events and provides exact timings for each of them. Thus the composition mixed a traditional musical instrument for solo recital, the piano, with more practical 'machines' for sound (re)production: some imitative of nature (birdsong, water) and others more domestic (scanning stations on the radio as well as shuffling playing cards above the piano strings). While 'Water Music' might be described as a more restrained version of a Futurist sound-noise performance, it was the second piece on that evening in 1952 which would become the artist's signature composition: '4′33″'. (On this first night it was called 'Four Pieces' and only later assigned the now more familiar title.)

'4′33″' required Tudor to sit at the piano and open the musical score, then raise the lid to the keyboard, start a stopwatch and shut the lid; after 30 seconds, he reset the stopwatch – an action that was repeated again after another 2 minutes and 23 seconds, and once more after a further 1 minute and 40 seconds. The pianist described the piece as 'one of the most intense listening experiences you can have' (Hermes 2000). Every bit as radical as Marinetti's *serate* in Milan – and generating as much audience disapproval (although no violence) in its inaugural rendition – Cage's composition was received 'as a joke or some kind of avant-garde nose-thumbing' (Hermes 2000). Audience and critics alike demanded to know what was the intention behind Cage's silent piano.

Of course, while there was no audible rendition of music from Tudor on stage, the performance in its fullest sense was not silent. Sounds from the pianist's and the audience's movements and expression, as well as those from the contextual environment, filled the sonic gaps '4′33″' appeared to create in the auditorium. In the absence of the music expected, given the presence of piano and pianist, the slightest scrape of a chair, cough by an audience member, creak from a door or even wind in the trees outside the Maverick Concert Hall registered in the listener's consciousness. This was Cage's point. His composition was designed to retrieve the usually inaudible as both the subject and object of the audience's experience. On the one hand, this performance acknowledged that the noisy city (that had so excited Marinetti and the Futurists) had more or less erased the many subtle and muted sounds of life's more natural elements. On the other, it also revealed, and revised, the sonic component of what had become the conventional production-reception contract in the performance of classical music (and, indeed, theatre): the performer licensed to make sound and the audience disciplined to be silent.

The genesis of '4′33″' had come from a visit by Cage to an 'anechoic chamber' (literally: a room without echoes) at Harvard University. The chamber had been built for engineering tests and was designed to provide maximum isolation from outside noise or vibration. But, instead of the complete silence Cage had anticipated in his immersion in the chamber, he reported to the Harvard engineers that he had heard two sounds, one high and one low, while he was in the room: 'When I described them to the engineer in charge, he informed me that the high one was my nervous system in operation, the low one my blood in circulation. Until I die there will be sounds' (Cage 1961: 8). And it was those sounds of the living body, not an all-encompassing condition of silence, that Cage wanted to capture in '4′33″' for his audiences. (In another kind of exploration of the living body, Shannon Yee's immersive audio performance, *Reassembled, Slightly Askew* (2015), puts audience members 'inside' the brain injury she suffered. This work will be discussed in Section Three.)

Eschewing the commonplace description of '4′33″' as silent performance, Ross Brown more accurately describes it as 'framed noise' (2010: 46). This is a helpful description since the composition requires of its audiences 'to let themselves go with the unintended and previously unattended sounds of silence to be found in their environment' (Ovadija 2016: 142). As a performance installation, '4′33″' prompts audiences to attend to whatever varieties of sound fill the void left by the noiseless piano and, more crucially, to think about how they hear them. Cage's composition is, in effect, another meditation on listening. It is timely, then, to return to Barthes's examination of the topic: he insisted that 'listening is active, it assumes the responsibility of taking its place in the interplay of desire, of which all language is the theater: we must repeat, *listening speaks*' (1977, Barthes 1985: 259). Experimental performance, Barthes argued, relied on signifying rather than signification (active meaning-making, not coded message). To elaborate this theory, he turned to Cage's work and described the specific experience of listening that this kind of composition demands: '[I]t is each sound one after the next that I listen to, not in its syntagmatic extension, but in its raw and as though vertical *signifying*: by deconstructing itself, listening is externalized, it compels the subject to renounce his "inwardness"' (1977, Barthes 1985: 259). As an exercise in listening, '4'33"' puts the relationship between sound-silence and the ear at the forefront of reception.

Cage's composition also acted, in its published form, as a challenge to the conventional method of writing for future sound (re)production. Typically a musical score deploys standard notation: language and symbols that not only furnish the content of the work but also serve as a guide to its realization in performance. But Cage's score deliberately parodied traditional practice and dismantled its authority. For the score of '4'33"', each of the three sections bears the instruction 'TACET' and notes the assigned duration so as to comprise the four minutes and 33 seconds of 'playing' time. 'Tacet' (Latin: literally 'it is silent') conventionally 'informs a player that he [sic] should play nothing during a movement' (Nyman 2008: 210); thus Cage's score repeats a conventional notation precisely to refuse the conventional realization of that notation (production of sound). Moreover, in the '4'33"' score, a 'secondary part of the notation tells the performer that the piece may be done on any instrument, for any length of time' (Nyman 2008: 210), destabilizing the authority of the original performance (and its printed remnant) and, at the same time, liberating future productions from apparent obligation to fidelity. Salomé Vogelin suggests that Cage here dematerialized 'the object of composition, emptying the score of its musical sounds' but, at the same time, trapping the new sounds perceived 'in the tight space of musical conventions and expectations' (2010: 81) – a problem, inevitably, for much avant-garde performance that was realized in concert halls, theatres and other culturally over-coded spaces.

Cage had signalled his interest in theorizing the sonic environment as early as 1937 in a short manifesto presented to the Seattle arts society. His subject was 'The Future of Music: Credo'. The talk was later published in the programme for a twenty-fifth anniversary retrospective of the artist's work in New York (1958) and is the first item in Cage's collected writings, a volume the author wryly called *Silence*. 'The Future of Music' begins: 'Wherever we are, what we hear is mostly noise. When we ignore it, it disturbs us. When we listen to it, we find it fascinating. The sound of a truck at fifty miles per hour. Static between the stations. Rain' (1961: 3). The 'fascinating' soundscape that he hears is different from, more diverse than, the urban noises that excited the Futurists. Like them, he drew on the sounds of transportation (a truck) and of new technologies (the radio), but, unlike them, he included the natural world (rain), suggesting a more holistic view of contemporary sonic possibilities. Furthermore, Cage continued to theorize the possibilities of sound production and wrote in 1957: 'Where do we go from here? Towards theatre. That art more than music resembles nature' (1961: 12).

The theatre Cage imagined, however, was not performing a repertoire of the classics of the Western dramatic canon. In fact, he expressed dismay at the plays of Shakespeare, Ibsen, Tennessee Williams he had seen, claiming in this context that 'the theater was a great disappointment to anybody interested in the arts' (Kostelanetz 1991: 24). Rather, he looked to the experimental performance scene of 1950s New York – for example, the Merce Cunningham Dance Company and The Living Theater. To accompany the latter's 1951–52 season at the Cherry Lane Theatre in Greenwich Village, Judith Malina and Julian Beck, the company's founders, asked Cage to write a manifesto. His very short document, with the single word headers 'instantaneous' and 'unpredictable', comprised:

nothing is accomplished by writing a piece of music) our ears are
)
"   "   "   " hearing "   "   "   "   )   now
)
"   "   "   " playing "   "   "   "   ) in excellent
                                                                                                condition.

(Cage 1961: xii)

These must have been inspiring precepts for the theatre that would introduce European playwrights such as Cocteau to New York audiences as well as stage the plays of American Modernists such as Gertrude Stein. Thus, Cage's ideas about sound, noise and silence emerged through his knowledge of, and often collaborations with, other artists living and working in New York at the same time – Merce Cunningham, Robert Rauschenberg, Beck and Malina, among them. In their different artistic disciplines (Cunningham in dance, Rauschenberg in the visual arts, Beck and Malina in theatre, Cage in music) each looked to create and practice anti-hierarchical and anarchical forms of artistic production and reception.

In 2008, visual artist Tacita Dean and Merce Cunningham collaborated on 'Stillness', a performance choreographed to Cage's '4'33"' where Cunningham held a pose, 'shifting positions for each of the three movements in Cage's composition' (Dean 2010). Cunningham, by then almost ninety years old, had been Cage's partner and frequent collaborator and 'Stillness' proved an elegant companion piece to a work still resonant after more than fifty years. '4'33"' nonetheless remains haunted by its designation as a silent work, a fact that underscores the awkward social space that soundlessness occupies. R. Murray Schafer (whose theories of environmental sound open Section Three) points out that 'the ultimate silence is death' and, in Western society, 'silence is negative, an embarrassment, a vacuum. Silence for Western man [sic] equals communication hang-up. If one does not speak, the other will speak' (2008: 37) – a theoretical position that the absent presence of the woman's telephonic interlocutor acted out in *The Human Voice*. Conventional rules of theatregoing prescribe silent behaviour for the audience – captured even before the performance proper begins in the injunction to turn off our mobile phones. These rules ensure the audience's attentiveness to sound emanating from the stage so much so that silence on stage often produces anxiety on the part of those who watch and listen. When no sound emanates from the performance proper, as in the case of Cage's '4'33"', non-intentional environmental noises inevitably fill the auditorium but this kind of enacted 'silence' has the capacity to create an unwilling self-consciousness in the audience member *qua* audience member, both individually and collectively. (A similar experience can come from an unexpected pause when an actor has forgotten lines.) Imposed 'silence', like the experience of the anechoic chamber that Cage visited, reveals the presence and existence of bodies. In its simplest form, that wordless sound of life is breath.

Samuel Beckett's brief play 'Breath' (written in 1969), like Cage's earlier experiment with '4′33″', strips performance of its most conventional elements – bodies and words. Instead Beckett's thirty-second piece uses only recorded sound and, resembling the structure of the Cage composition, presents that sound in strictly time-choreographed, distinct sequences. 'Breath' has three 'acts': the first describes the stage, faintly lit and 'littered with miscellaneous rubbish' with an instruction to hold the tableau for five seconds (1971: 9). The second reads: 'Faint brief cry and immediately inspiration and slow increase of light together reaching maximum together in about ten seconds. Silence and hold about five seconds' (1971: 9). The final segment indicates 'Expiration and slow decrease of light together reaching minimum together' over a ten-second period until the light level matches that at the start of the play (1971: 9). 'Breath' ends with five seconds of silence. The additional instructions that the script provides are equally minimalist and quite precise on the subject sound: the two cries must be identical, the sound of 'vagitus' (*OED*: 'A cry or wail; *spec*. that of a new-born child'). Further, Beckett prescribes that the cries and breathing should be derived from recorded sound and not performed live. With garbage lying all around the playing space, the audience is literally looking at rubbish – nothing of value – but impelled to listen to something of remarkable value, the breath that sustains all human life punctuated by those first sounds that indicate every individual's viable entry into the world.

'Breath' was originally written for inclusion in Kenneth Tynan's erotic revue *O! Calcutta!* in New York, on the understanding that the pieces commissioned would be performed anonymously. Other luminaries such as John Lennon and Sam Shepard also contributed. Beckett's short script (he sent it to Tynan on the back of a postcard) was presented on the opening night of the revue with naked bodies writhing in the garbage-strewn setting and with Beckett's authorship attached. Because of these two departures from the agreement with Tynan, Beckett angrily withdrew 'Breath' from the production. Later in the same year, 'Breath' received a theatrical premiere in Glasgow. As part of a project to record all of Beckett's stage plays, a film version of 'Breath' was made in 2001, directed by Damien Hirst.

Acousmatics and radiophonics: Pierre Schaeffer and the BBC

Performance of the absent body was, by 1969, already well practiced in Beckett's oeuvre through the sequence of dramas he wrote for BBC radio in the late 1950s and in his well-known stage play *Krapp's Last Tape* (1958), a dialogue between the onstage actor and tape-recorded diary entries. If the gramophone and telephone had become familiar performance technologies in the first decades of the twentieth century, by the 1950s interest had moved on to new forms of sound recording that Beckett, among others, was keen to explore. And an ascendant performance platform was, at this time, the radio. As Tim Crook notes in his study of the genre, radio drama 'had a short period when it floated in the luxury of radio as an electronic medium that was dominant for about thirty years' (1922–52) (1999: 49).

Beckett, living in Paris, was almost certainly aware of the work of radio engineer and sound theorist Pierre Schaeffer; moreover, the radio drama team at the BBC who commissioned Beckett's radio plays had been to the French capital to visit Schaeffer's sound studio and were keen to test out his theories through their productions of Beckett's work. Schaeffer's theory of acousmatics, fifteen years in the making and eventually to appear in published form in 1966 as *Traité des objets musicaux (Treatise on Musical Objects)*, addressed the reception of sound when its source could not been seen – as in the case of radio transmission. The *OED* provides two definitions of 'acousmatics', collectively an illustration of both the history behind Schaeffer's selection of the term and the more recent meaning that his own theory had introduced. In the historical sense, 'acousmatics' was the term given to the students of ancient Greek philosopher-mathematician Pythagoras; from Schaefferian theory, the word became 'of, designating, or characterized by sound produced without a visible source, a visual component or association; audible but unseen'.

So why did Schaeffer turn to Pythagoras for his terminology? As the *OED* explains, this was 'owing to the belief that the acousmatic followers of Pythagoras were so called because they were not permitted to see Pythagoras when they listened to his lectures'. As a disembodied source of sound – Pythagoras stood behind a curtain and demanded his students remained on the other side in total and respectful silence – the ancient Greek philosopher-mathematician was a useful figure for Schaeffer's theoretical imperative: to describe what was 'audible but unseen' but also to understand how audiences listen in such circumstances. Schaeffer writes:

> This is why we can, without anachronism, return to an ancient tradition which, no less nor otherwise than contemporary radio and recordings, gives back to the ear alone the entire responsibility of a perception that ordinarily rests on other sensible witnesses. In ancient times, the apparatus was a curtain; today, it is the radio and the methods of reproduction, along with the whole set of electro-acoustic transformations, that place, us, modern listeners to an invisible voice, under similar conditions. (2008: 77)

As this extract illustrates, Schaeffer's interest in the reception of sound followed a phenomenological approach, drawing specifically on the work of German philosopher Edmund Husserl. Indeed, to establish the phenomenological basis for his own theory, Schaeffer quoted at length from Husserl's *Ideas*:

> Let us start with an example. Constantly seeing this table and meanwhile walking around it, changing my position in space in whatever way, I have continually the consciousness of this one identical table as factually existing 'in person' and remaining quite unchanged. The table-perception, however, is a continually changing one; it is a continuity of changing perceptions. I close my eyes. My other senses have no relation to the table. Now I have no perception of it. I open my eyes; and I have the perception again. *The* perception? Let us be more precise. Returning, it is not, under any circumstances, individually the same. Only the table is the same, intended to as the same in the synthetical consciousness which connects the new perception with the memory .... The perception itself, however, is what it is in the continuous flux of consciousness and is itself a continuous flux: continually the perceptual Now changes into the enduring consciousness of the Just-Past and simultaneously a new Now lights up, etc. The perceived thing in general, and all its parts, aspects, and phases ... are necessarily transcendent to the perception. (cited in Schaeffer 2017: 207)

In other words, perception is not what the thing is or means but rests in the experience of the thing and in the content/meaning produced by that experience of the thing. If Husserl's elaboration was singularly visual, how, Schaeffer wondered, could this be articulated in the context of sound production?

The answer was to be found in his description of a 'sonorous object' that must first be defined by what it is not. It is not the instrument that was actually played (the source of the sound) nor was it the gramophone record or tape (the acoustic signal); rather, the sonorous object was *'contained entirely in our perceptive consciousness'* (2008: 79, emphasis in original). For this reason, a sonorous object is only revealed in the acousmatic experience. As Brian Kane explains, 'Schaeffer understands the Pythagorean veil (and its perpetuation in the form of modern audio technology) as a tool for bracketing the spatiotemporal factuality of the sonic source. This encourages two fundamental changes: first, the objectivity of sound is grasped as a phenomenon, and second, attention is redirected to the particular essential characteristics of a given sound' (2014: 25). Schaeffer termed this experience acousmatic or 'reduced' listening, the perception of sound apart from its source. In other words, his theory was a perfect match to the practice of listening invoked by the increasingly popular medium of radio.

As Schaeffer explained it, in the practice of reduced listening, 'sound no longer appears as a medium or placeholder for "some other thing"' (Kane 2014: 29), excluding – in the same ways that Husserl had described for his object table – 'other sensory means of assessing sound' (Kane 2014: 37). 'Such is the suggestion of acoustmatics', Schaeffer wrote, 'to deny the instrument and cultural conditioning, *to put in front of us the sonorous and its musical "possibility"*' (2008: 81, emphasis in original). Schaeffer was himself a sound composer, of what he called *musique concrète* (concrete music), a fertile ground for testing his theories of sonorous objects and reduced listening. In 1948, he had produced a 'concert of noises' for broadcast on French radio, 'a set of pieces composed entirely from recordings of train whistles, spinning tops, pots and pans, canal boats, percussion instruments, and the occasional piano' (Cox and Warner 2008: 5). His composition had been later released on gramophone records – a set of which the BBC radio team brought back to London after their visit to Schaeffer's Paris studio.

It is not surprising, then, to find in the first of Beckett's radio plays, *All That Fall* (first presented on BBC's Third Programme on 13 January 1957), sonically dense stage directions that actualize Schaeffer's conception of the sonorous object. The script of *All That Fall* opens:

> *Rural sounds. Sheep, bird, cow, cock,*
> *severally then together.*
> *Silence.*
> *Mrs. Rooney advances along country road*
> *towards railway-station. Sound of her*
> *dragging feet.*
> *Music faint from house by way. 'Death and*
> *the Maiden.' The steps slow own, stop.*
>
> MRS. ROONEY
> Poor woman. All alone in that ruinous old
> house.
> *Music louder. Silence but for music playing.*
> *The steps resume. Music dies. Mrs. Rooney*
> *murmurs melody. Her murmur dies.*
> *Sound of approaching cartwheels. The*
> *cart stops The steps slow down, stop.* (Beckett 1981: 33)

What Beckett provided for radio performance were not directions for a naturalistic scene, a slice of rural Irish life; rather, he described the soundscape produced by, and existing in, the consciousness of Mrs. Rooney on her walk to the railway station. Donald McWhinnie, at the time Assistant Head of Drama at the BBC's Third Programme and one of the group who had visited Radiodiffusion-Télévision Française's sound laboratory where Schaeffer held a senior position, met with Beckett to discuss 'the acoustic design of the play, and both agreed that the sound should be treated surrealistically in order to evoke the inner life of Maddy Rooney' (Porter 2010: 440). To this end, rather than deploy actual sounds from their effects library (for example, the sheep, bird, cow and cock with which the play starts), the director asked the actors to voice them – a decision with which Beckett expressed some dissatisfaction (Morin 2014: 9).

Elsewhere in the design for *All That Fall*, the production team at the BBC did elect to use sounds from their extensive sound library but brought the sought-after 'surreal' quality to their delivery by means of electronic manipulation. Some pre-recorded sounds were slowed down or speeded up. Other sounds were re-recorded on tape, allowing them to be spliced into segments and reassembled in a different order. These innovations in sound production designed specifically for *All That Fall* proved to be a crucial step towards the BBC's creation, a year later, of the Radiophonic Workshop (where, among other things, the theme for *Doctor Who* was first created). But, as Everett Frost points out, techniques of sound manipulation that were groundbreaking in radio dramas of the 1950s have since 'become the clichés of the popular music recording industry and commercial advertising' (1991: 370).

In the BBC production, to emphasize that events in *All That Fall* were to be heard as the process of Mrs. Rooney's perception, the actor (Mary O'Farrell) was placed in close proximity to the recording microphone while the other speakers were kept further away. 'Across the airwaves', as Jeff Porter suggests, 'Maddy [Rooney] looms large. In contrast with the other, more muted characters, she is heard as an expressive subject who fills up the air space. Not surprisingly, it was much easier for Beckett to erase the boundary between subject and object on the radio than on the stage' (2010: 442). In effect, the play created for its listeners, *pace* Schaeffer, Maddy Rooney's sonorous body. After the play's enthusiastic reception by critics and listeners alike, there was considerable interest in putting it on stage – an idea that Beckett abhorred:

> *All That Fall* is specifically a radio play, or rather radio text, for voices, not bodies. I have already refused to have it 'staged' and I cannot think of it in such terms .... I am absolutely opposed to any form of adaptation with a view to its conversion into 'theatre'. It is no more theatre than

> *End-Game* is radio and to 'act' it is to kill it. (quoted in Frost 1991: 366)

Knowledge of Beckett's outrage about collapsing the distinctions between the reception of radio drama and stage plays – as well as knowledge of Schaeffer's theory of reduced listening – might animate new questions for more contemporary performance including the PlayMe podcast and many examples of headphone theatre.

'*All That Fall* provided both a context and an outlet for the BBC's exploration of the new territories opened up by the magnetic tape' (2014: 2) and the 'acoustic sophistication of Beckett's script', Emilie Morin suggests, 'marked a decisive turning point for the BBC's work on radiophonic sound' (2014: 2). While this is undoubtedly true, writing for the sound-only medium of radio drama appears to have been an experience that prompted Beckett to think more about the dramatic potentials of new technologies of sound and, specifically, about the usability of magnetic tape. The result was the play that received its first production, directed by Donald McWhinnie, at London's Royal Court Theatre in October 1958: *Krapp's Last Tape*.

One of Beckett's most regularly produced dramas, *Krapp's Last Tape* is, like Cocteau's *The Human Voice*, a dialogue with the unseen other. In the play, an old man (it appears to be his sixty-ninth birthday) listens to, and interacts with, a tape-recorded diary entry he had made on his thirty-ninth birthday (where he talks about previous recordings made 'ten or twelve years ago' [1981: 16]); he then attempts, quite unsuccessfully, to record a new entry to capture the present occasion. *Krapp's Last Tape* takes up two theoretical problems that had circulated around the increasing importance that technologies of sound recording and reproduction assumed in social, political and cultural contexts: what, in these circumstances, was 'original' sound and how should we understand the impact of sound's addition to the archive?

Aura and archive: Making sound memories

To prepare for Beckett's theatrical unpicking of these two theoretical concerns, this section rewinds first to demonstrations of the telephone and phonograph in the late nineteenth and early twentieth centuries and then to the promise of the sound archive that new recording technologies had created.

From the outset, the telephone and the phonograph were deployed in performance and, as Jonathan Sterne describes, Alexander Graham Bell and Thomas Watson travelled around the United States to exhibit their invention 'with Bell demonstrating the virtues of the phone and Watson performing (and managing other performers) on the other end of the line' (2003: 250). The *théâtrephone*, discussed earlier in this section, had its first demonstrations at the 1881 World Exposition in Paris where visitors lined up to hear snippets of a performance from the Comédie-Française. In the next decades, phonograph parlours sprung up across the United States where customers took up a 'hearing tube' from a coin-operated machine to 'listen to a short tune or sketch' (Sterne 2003: 162). Other phonographic entertainments were more temporary – for example, a street corner where photographs and a hearing-tube-equipped phonograph might be set up for a small group of people to view and then listen. Gustavus Stadler recounts a horrifying example of one such entertainment as it was described by a 'prominent African American entrepreneur, veterinarian, civic leader, Civil War veteran, and anti-lynching activist Samuel Burdett' who was visiting the city of Seattle in 1893 (2010b: 88).

Burdett had unwittingly come across the street-corner installation of a photograph and wax-cylinder phonographic 'entertainment' that purported to record a lynching in Paris, Texas, of one Henry Smith:

The helpless victim almost went mad at the very thought of being tortured as he saw he was going to be. He hollered out in an agonizing, heart-rending manner, 'Oh, Lord, Mr. –,for God's sake don't burn me; Don't burn me – Oh, oh, kill me, kill me! Shoot me, shoot me!' His crying and entreaties fell on deaf ears. Hot irons were brought out, and then his eyes were burned out. The moans and screams which he uttered cannot be described, and perhaps it is as well that they cannot. It were better that it all might be forgotten, and that nothing of the same character should ever transpire again. The things seen and heard there have haunted the writer from that day to this. (2010b: 89)

The traveller's vivid description of his listening experience suggests the affective power of recorded sound performance; after all, he dwells on the sounds of Smith, not the images of the torture on display. But, as Stadler goes on to explain, the likelihood that Burdett was listening to an authentic recording of the actual event was slim to none. At this time, recording technology was generally confined to the studio and even if the lynching of Smith had been thoroughly premeditated, 'it would have been essentially impossible to encapsulate on a phonographic cylinder in any manner approaching the completeness and "fidelity"' that Barrett's account describes (Stadler 2010b: 92). What is much more likely, then, is that this was a recreated performance of the lynching event, undertaken in studio for the purpose of its future commercial circulation. In this context, Stadler describes the catalogue of The Talking Machine Company of Chicago: among its many offerings was the 'Burning of Smith at Paris, Texas', listed as the creation of one of the company's most popular artists, Silas Leachman.

Other catalogue items ranged from spectacular events (such as the San Francisco earthquake of 1906 and the departure of a Hamburg–America ocean liner) to mashups of scenes from Harriet Beecher Stowe's *Uncle Tom's Cabin* complete with minstrel songs. These sound recordings, then, were intended to work as street performances that 'advertised to listeners the affective and aesthetic potential of the medium' and promised 'listeners kinds of experiences not previously available to them' (Sterne 2003: 242). Very few wax cylinders exist today and only very few of those few that do are readily playable, but Stadler is surely correct in his conclusion that the street-corner performance that Burdett stumbled over was 'part of a growing culture industry in sound recordings' that captured all kinds of events 'in a highly theatricalized form' (2010b: 95). This slice of sonic history is relevant, too, for its anticipation of 'headphone theatre' – a popular performance genre more than a hundred years later and a topic for the final section of this book.

Examples of how new sound technologies found a market both through and as performance connect to the concerns of Walter Benjamin's well-known essay, 'The Work of Art in the Age of Mechanical Reproduction' (1936). He writes: 'Around 1900 technical reproduction had reached a standard that ... permitted it to reproduce all transmitted works of art and thus to cause the most profound change in their impact upon the public' (2008: 36). The advent of new technologies, importantly for Benjamin, rewrote the relationship between original and copy. As he notes, manual reproduction of an original was generally designated less than – indeed, 'a forgery' – and this belief allowed the original to maintain its authority: 'not so *vis à vis* technical reproduction' which 'can put the copy of the original into situations which would be out of reach for the original itself' (2008: 36). To illustrate, Benjamin suggested that the phonograph record could deliver an original performance into a home's drawing room.

Thus, the power of mechanical reproduction, Benjamin argued, lay in its ability to change 'the reaction of the masses toward art' (2008: 45). The distribution of technically accurate copies caused the 'aura' of the original to wither and a possibility of politics to take up the vacated space. Notwithstanding what Benjamin sees here as the more accessible 'copy', Jonathan Sterne has argued for a much more careful theorization of the specific conditions underlying sound reproduction: 'Without the technology of reproduction, the copies do not exist, but, then, neither would the originals. A philosophy of mediation ontologizes sound reproduction too quickly' (2003: 219). Sterne's contention is that, in the field of sound, distinctions between original and copy 'operate as placeholders for concerns about the social process of sound reproduction itself' (2003: 221). In the original–copy dynamic inherent to sound recording, this has almost always been described as the quest for perfect fidelity.

Although, as Sterne notes, 'every age' of sound recording has had its own standard of 'perfect fidelity' (2003: 222), the most familiar image likely remains the one of Nipper the dog, leaning in to the horn of a phonograph at the sound of His Master's Voice. Implied in the advertisement (trademarked in 1900 and used for decades by the Victor and HMV companies) is, of course, the dog's inability to tell the difference between original and copy; for the master, however, it threatened the possibility of erasure. Understanding the dynamic of this sound-ear equation, Sterne suggests that the fantasy of perfect fidelity demands 'a loss of being, the disappearance of aura' (2003: 285). Sound recording portends a precarious subjectivity, then – a condition that *Krapp's Last Tape* examines in the stage presentation of a protagonist who appears in both live and recorded form.

The second prompt necessary to prepare, theoretically speaking, for Beckett's tape recorder play comes from the entry of sound into archival collections. The advent of new recording technologies late in the nineteenth century offered the possibility of extending archival evidence beyond artefact and text. For the first time, it would be possible to preserve, and later hear, events from the past and, more significantly, voices beyond the grave. As Sterne notes, 'The chance to hear "the voices of the dead" as a figure of the possibilities of sound recording appears with morbid regularity in technical descriptions, advertisements, announcements, circulars, philosophical speculations, and practical descriptions' (2003: 289). While much of this discourse was devised in order to market the new sound recording machines commercially, the appeal of this 'resonant tomb' was vast (Sterne 2003: 287). Future generations, whether in a domestic setting or a national archive, could theoretically have access to actual sonic evidence – another aspirational performance of fidelity.

But, in reality, sound preservation has proven difficult and unreliable: most of the earliest sound recordings held in archives cannot be played either because they are too fragile or because we no longer have access to the specific player for which they were designed. For example, the National Museum of American History (part of the Smithsonian) has in its collection about 400 of the earliest audio recordings made by Volta Laboratories, an enterprise run by Alexander Graham Bell and his partners. But, until a new technology was developed, no one at the museum had ever heard them. It had been deemed impossible without fatally damaging the historical artefacts. Only the development of a non-invasive optical process that created a high-resolution digital scan allowed, in 2011, for the 'sonification' of six of the discs in their collection ('Playback'). When these discs from the 1880s were eventually heard, it was likely for the first time in more than a century. One – of a man reciting the 'To be or not to be' speech from *Hamlet* – is almost certainly the earliest recording of a Shakespeare 'performance'. More and more theatre companies now archive their performances via video recording and the fate of the earliest sound recordings reminds us that modes of technology inevitably come with eventual obsolescence. Even as 'recently' as the late twentieth century, theatrical productions recorded on videotape have become, in some circumstances, unplayable and, even when the relevant machines are available for playback, recordings are often substantially degraded by both age and wear. Despite an exponentially growing digital archive replete with HD recordings of performances, we need to be cautious, surely, of what future acoustic archaeologists might be able to hear.

As phonograph records grew in popularity and affordability, many 'great' late nineteenth- and early twentieth-century actors recorded speeches from the plays that made them stage celebrities. These were intended for commercial sale, but they also changed the scope of, and expectation for, the archive informing theatre history. Some of the cylinders from the late 1890s have survived and offer recordings of Sir Henry Irving, Ellen Terry, Edwin Booth and Herbert Beerbohm Tree performing speeches from the Shakespeare plays in which they had famously appeared. What can we learn about the conventions of nineteenth-century performance from listening to these voices? What can we learn about the history of Shakespearean performance in that time that might open new questions for performances before and since? Is the style of delivery for these well-known speeches representative or exceptional for late nineteenth-century performance? We might remind ourselves of Maarten Walraven's exploration of the 'audibility' of history; as he put it, 'How does the historian turn into a listening historian?' (2013). And, even as these early examples of actors speaking Shakespeare miraculously exist, how many other late-nineteenth-century performances of the same Shakespearean roles have been lost? What archival silences remain? For example, the first broadcast of a Shakespeare play on BBC Radio, a 110-minute performance of *Twelfth Night* on the evening of 28 May 1923, has no known recording in existence (McMurty 2016).

Case study: Samuel Beckett's *Krapp's Last Tape*

In *Krapp's Last Tape*, Beckett explores the fidelity of the sonic archive as well as the actions of a listening historian. The protagonist (Krapp) has had the habit of tape recording a diary entry each year on the occasion of his birthday and, as archivist of his own life, listing each spool of tape and a brief summary of its contents in a ledger. In the course of the play, he seeks out a particular spool, one he recorded on his thirty-ninth birthday – apparently thirty years earlier, suggesting that 'today' is his sixty-ninth birthday – and attempts to record an entry for the immediately past year. The performance starts with an extended mime sequence, largely involving the eating of bananas and consumption of alcohol, before Krapp, '*a wearish old man*', finally speaks:

> KRAPP (*briskly*). Ah! (*He bends over ledger, turns the pages, finds the entry he wants, reads.*) Box ... thrree ... spool ... five. (*He raises his head and stares front. With relish.*) Spool! (*Pause.*) Spooool! (*Happy smile. Pause. He bends over table, starts peering and poking at the boxes.*) Box ... thrree ... thrree ... four ... two ... (*with surprise*) nine! Good God! ... seven ... ah! The little rascal! (1981: 12)

The combination of Beckett's phonetic instructions to the actor (such as the extended 'o' sound of 'Spooool') and his stage directions that signal specific affective responses imply the pleasure Krapp expects to find in his archival project. Krapp's sounds form a contrast to his decrepit physical condition that, as Jane Blocker suggests, 'lends urgency to the task of conserving the historical record' (2015: 41). Yet this man, whose birthday celebrations are both solitary and modest, seems to anthropomorphize his taped recollections as favourite companions as much as traces of his own past. If number seven is a 'little rascal', then spool five – the one he's been looking for – is a 'little scoundrel!' (1981: 12). The ledger's summary of spool five concludes 'Farewell to love' (1981: 13) and, at that point, Krapp '*raises his head, broods, bends over machine, switches on and assumes listening posture, i.e. leaning forward, elbows on table, hand cupping ear towards machine, face front*' (1981: 13). He is prepared to hear the acousmatic voice, speaking to him from the remote past. As Schaeffer's theory proposed, 'The tape recorder has the virtue of Pythagoras' curtain: if it creates new phenomena to observe, it creates above all new conditions of observation' (2008: 81).

The second character in *Krapp's Last Tape* is, then, Tape, whose words predominate in the thirty-minute drama. Like the telephonic almost-ex-lover of Cocteau's play, the taped 39-year-old Krapp proves a confident interlocutor. Stage directions indicate a '*strong voice, rather pompous*' (1981: 14) as his narrative reaches back into tales of his twenties – 'Hard to believe I was ever that young whelp! The voice! Jesus! And the aspirations! (*Brief laugh in which Krapp joins.*)' (1981: 16). He turns next to the deaths of his parents and, of his mother, where he comments 'there is of course the house on the canal where mother lay a-dying, in the late autumn, after her long viduity, and the – ' (1981: 18). At this point Krapp jumps up and then stops the tape. He rewinds, leans in to the tape recorder and replays that last phrase. The word 'viduity' puzzles him and he leaves the stage, to return almost immediately with '*an enormous dictionary*' (1981: 18) that provides him with the word's meaning, knowledge that has evidently dissipated with the passing years. A single word from the sound archive has the capacity to undo Krapp's sense of self. A little later, Krapp starts the present year's recording with a reflection on his spool five self: 'Just been listening to that stupid bastard I took myself for thirty years ago, hard to believe I was ever as bad as that. Thank God that's all done with anyway' (1981: 24). Here Beckett surely asserts a necessary scepticism in claims for the fidelity of sound recording ('hard to believe') and the promise of the archive.

Moreover, Krapp's attempt to record a new entry is largely unsuccessful: 'Nothing to say, not a squeak. What's a year now? The sour cud and the iron stool. (*Pause.*) Revelled in the word spool. (*With relish.*) Spooool! Happiest moment of the past half million' (1981: 25). From this flash of sonic pleasure, he moves to a summary of his 'success' as an author: 'Seventeen copies sold, of which eleven at trade price to free circulating libraries beyond the seas. Getting known' (1981: 25). Rather than the somewhat hopeful 'Getting known', however, Krapp's print output might more accurately gesture towards Jacques Derrida's suggestion that the development of 'phonography and of all the means of conserving the spoken language, of making it function without the presence of the speaking subject' might portend the end of the book (1976: 10).

Krapp's attempt to make a new recording continues with fragmentary thoughts that drift from one topic to the next, from the present reality to his childhood, from lovers desired to lovers lost, before he abruptly switches off the recorder. He removes the tape and replaces it with spool five, again, and hits fast forward to reach its conclusion:

> Here I end this reel. Box – (*pause*) – three, spool – (*pause*) – five. (*Pause.*) Perhaps my best years are gone. When there was a chance of happiness. But I wouldn't want them back. Not with the fire in me now. No, I wouldn't want them back.
>
> *Krapp motionless staring before him. The tape runs on in silence.*
>
> CURTAIN
>
> (1981: 28)

The character's listening posture, along with his failed attempt to capture his 'now', suggests that these recordings form an endless, and eventually soundless, chronicle of his life. Krapp bemoans the passing of his 'best years', even as the tapes preserve them in sonic form. Neither the 39-year-old nor the 69-year-old Krapp wants those years back but neither is comfortable with his present moment. Derval Turbidy posits the archive of tape recordings as 'a technological revetment against the erosion of memory by time' (2007: 5). But, as Krapp's wrestling with the word 'viduity' demonstrates, sound traces of his younger years have not effectively maintained and protected his memory. Perhaps Sterne's expression is closer to the truth: that is, Krapp's tapes are a 'resonant tomb'. But, perhaps not, since the very first stage direction in *Krapp's Last Tape* indicates '*A late evening in the future*' (1981: 9). With such an ambiguous sense of the play's time, Krapp's history is unclear and his sonic archive's provenance uncertain. If this is indeed Krapp's last tape, what remains?

The theories and practices of sound that characterized avant-garde performance across the first half of the twentieth century illustrate both the rapid development of new technologies and the incorporation of their diffuse potentials into theatrical practices. What had started out as experimental, opening up live performance to an array of new possibilities for sound production became, in the century's second half, a standard part of theatrical practice. Assumptions about the dramatic potentials of sound, noise, silence and different manners of listening finally migrated from avant-garde performance to the theatrical mainstream. As director Peter Sellars put it, 'Very late in our day, the technology has become available to allow sound to begin to occupy the place in theatre arts that it occupies in our lives' (2013).

By the 1970s, as Christopher Baugh further explains, sound designers were charged with 'the creation and constant modulation of the entire auditory experience of a performance' (2013: 208) – elements that became ever more sophisticated and even easier to manage and manipulate with computer-based technology. In this context, Lynne Kendrick observes that 'the designer is no longer necessarily confined to a specific space, to certain times in the production process, or indeed to a received idea of what the sound designer role should be' (2017: xix).

And, to quote Sellars again,

> We are beyond the era of sound 'effects'. Sound is no longer an effect, an extra, a *garni* supplied from time to time to mask a scene change or ease a transition. We are beyond the era of door buzzers and thunderclaps. Or rather, door buzzers and thunderclaps are no longer isolated effects, but part of a total program of sound that speaks to theatre as ontology. Sound is the holistic process and program that binds our multifarious experience of the world. Sound

is our own inner continuity track. It is also our primary outward gesture to the world, our first and best chance to communicate with others, to become part of a larger rhythm. (2013)

The final section of this book continues to recognize and evaluate the impact of new technologies on sound performance. The advent of increasingly mobile technologies has not only produced what Michael Bull calls 'iPod culture' (2013a: 526) but also richly enabled experiential performance, a practice that hails the audience as co-creator of this participatory form. The relative affordability of these new technologies (at least in the context of the developed world) has, as we shall see, enabled more inclusive sound economies and new acoustic world-makings to emerge.

SECTION THREE

Experiential Sound

Prosthetic performance and deterritorialized listening

The final section of *Sound* addresses sonic practices enabled by the late twentieth-century development of new mobile technologies – innovations that both open up new sonic possibilities in the theatre and accelerated the movement of performance out of conventional theatre buildings into found spaces, both indoors and outside. Particularly, sound is the core medium for what we have come to call 'headphone theatre', a form Rosemary Klich defines as 'a sub-genre of the wider sphere of "immersive" theatre' and 'rooted within a digital performance paradigm that uses locative, wearable, audio, and mobile devices to facilitate immersive and intersensorial audience experiences' (2017: 366). In other words, headphone theatre relies on creating (and involving its audiences in) immersive performance soundscapes.

But before examining case study examples of these experiential sound theatres of the late twentieth- and early twenty-first centuries, we need to account for the advent of this concept of the soundscape. The term, used to capture all the elements of an acoustic environment, had its origins, in the late 1960s, in the research of a group led by R. Murray Schafer at Simon Fraser University in Canada. The group's work had, initially at least, been motivated to counteract burgeoning noise pollution in urban environments. In his well-known and influential pamphlet *The Music of the Environment* (1973), Schafer wrote: 'The soundscape of the world is changing. Modern man [sic] is beginning to inhabit a world with an acoustical environment radically different from any he has hitherto known' (2008: 29).

To explicate this notion of radical difference, Schafer's theory traces concepts of high- and low-fidelity (hi-fi/lo-fi) where a 'hi-fi soundscape is one in which discrete sounds can be heard clearly because of the low ambient noise level' and a lo-fi soundscape is one in which 'individual acoustic signals are obscured in an overdense population of sounds' (2008: 32). The soundscapes of cities, he suggested, were lo-fi, an inevitable by-product of industrialization and the same conditions, of course, that had earlier in the twentieth century inspired Russolo's noise orchestra and Schaeffer's *musique concrète*. Merging music with the auditory environment, the avant-garde practitioners had celebrated 'overdense' lo-fi sound. In contrast to his Modernist predecessors, however, Schafer privileged the hi-fi countryside and imagined an acoustic design that would 'let nature sing for itself' (2008: 36). The ever-increasing noise of modern life risked inhibiting – even silencing – natural sound and, thus, our humanity. This position Schafer explicitly linked to John Cage's theories of sound, and his own ideas were reminiscent of the environmental awareness that works like '4'33"' were intended to promote. By the mid-1970s, Schafer's research group had established the World Soundscape Project (WSP), conducting thick-description collection and analysis of relationships between people and their acoustic environments. To this end, they worked on the soundscapes of five villages – one each in Sweden, Germany, France, Italy and Scotland. An archive of acoustic world-making, the WSP sought to address a lacuna in conventional field anthropology (where sound recording is conventionally considered a methodology and not content) so as to think about sound as 'a publicly circulating entity that is a produced effect of social practices, politics, and ideologies while also being implicated in the shaping of those practices, politics and ideologies' (Samuels et al. 2010: 330).

More generally in his work, Schafer advocated for the promotion and preservation of a hi-fi acoustic world – nostalgia, surely, for pre-industrial societies and a simpler appreciation of their human-scaled soundscapes. In fact, Schafer's language, in 1973, was not so very different from Bacon's in *Sylva Sylvarum* where that seventeenth-century study of sound paid attention to the 'hidden portions of Nature' (Bacon 1626: 23). Nonetheless, Schafer's idea of a soundscape has been profoundly influential across disciplinary and interdisciplinary thinking about all kinds of sonic practices (it is a key term in Sound Studies scholarship) and as an inspiration and guide for the development of sound art.

Where Schafer's theory of an acoustic ecology better prepares us for thinking through contemporary practices of experiential performance is, specifically, in his dissection of listening spaces. In an explication of sound reception, Schafer articulated a spectrum of conditions that ran from the 'concentrated listening' encouraged by a dedicated theatre or concert space via the 'peripheral hearing' possible at an outdoor performance (think here of the 'broad' sound that Bruce Smith described for Shakespeare's Globe) to headphone listening which isolates 'the listener in a private acoustic space' (2008: 35). For Schafer, headphone listening initiated a dynamically new and individualized experience within its contextual sonic environment:

> [W]hen sound is conducted directly through the skull of the headphone listener, he [*sic*] is no longer regarding events on the acoustic horizon; no longer is he surrounded by a sphere of moving elements. He is the sphere. He is universe. While most twentieth-century developments in sound production tend to fragment the listening experience and break up concentration, headphone listening directs the listener towards a new integrity with himself. (2008: 35–6)

In other words, headphone sound orchestrated the listener at the centre of the world in which the acoustic experience took place, creating for 'him' a narcissistic performance of the self. Headphone technology, Schafer argued, made the listening experience complete and singular as it affirmed the listening subject.

On 1 July 1979, the Japanese electronics company Sony introduced the first portable magnetic tape cassette player, battery-powered and equipped with a headphone jack but no external speaker. Its first American name was the 'Sound-About' but the device soon became known globally as the 'Walkman'. Sony had optimistically projected sales of 5,000 units a month, but remarkably more than 50,000 were sold in the first two months (Haire 2009). The freedom that the Walkman allowed, not surprisingly, soon piqued the interest of both performance artists and sound theorists. Shuhei Hosokawa's 1984 landmark essay 'The Walkman Effect' gives some sense of what this technology made available, for the first time, to users.

Hosokawa took up what he saw as the limits of Schafer's theory of headphone listening as an isolated space, applying Gilles Deleuze and Félix Guattari's notion of 'territorialization' to suggest the conservatism implicit in Schafer's thinking. By contrast, for Hosokawa, 'walkman listening on the street appears as "deterritorialised listening"' (1984: 175). In other words, while Schafer's concept of headphone listening was, for Hosokawa, no more than the latest iteration of a traditionally conceived and constricted practice, the Walkman, he argued, deterritorialized that process. Hosokawa understood the potential of the Walkman to dismantle architectures of control as well as to disarticulate codes of sonic reception: 'You may ask yourself how the Walkman, while making no substantial contribution to the public soundscape, can intervene in the urban tone, how it can interfere with the urban acoustic without having a material effect. The answer is: through the *walk act*' (1984: 175, emphasis in original).

The pleasure and the promise of the Walkman came, as Hosokawa saw it, precisely in the mashup performance of listening and moving. Audiences in theatres and concert halls might be expected to practice what Schafer had called 'concentrated listening' (Hosokawa calls it subtractional listening – where the audience typically commits to participate in the active elimination of all sounds except those of the focus performance), but the Walkman allowed for 'an *additional* listening act' (1984: 176, emphasis in original) for which the sound-generating instrument performed as prosthetic. Hosokawa's description of the bodily sensations that additional listening produced carries, rather ironically, an echo of Cage's immersive experience in Harvard's anechoic chamber:

> When we listen to the 'beat' of our body, when the walkman intrudes inside the skin, the order of our body is inverted, that is, the surface tension of the skin loses its balancing function through which it activates the interpenetration of Self and world: a *mise en oeuvre* in the body, through the body, of the body .... Through the walkman, the body is opened; it is put into the process of the aestheticisation, the theatricalisation of the urban – but *in secret*. (1984: 177, emphasis in original)

Thus Hosokawa celebrated the Walkman as a 'secret theatre' (1984: 177), intrinsically open, mobile and embodied. He argued that passers-by recognize the performance of the actor (the holder of the performance-instrument) but cannot know its content.

Similarly, Iain Chambers described the Walkman as 'a privileged object of contemporary nomadism', encouraging in its users a Benjaminian *flânerie* inflected with emotional energy and musical beat (1984: 99). Succinctly, and following Hosokawa's dramatic metaphors, Chambers argued that 'the Walkman is both a mask and a masque: a quiet putting into act of localised theatrics' (1984: 99). As a sound technology consistently defined by a theatrical vocabulary, it is hardly surprising that the Walkman became, more literally, an occasion for performance creation that put the bodies of the audience to work. 'Experiential sound' will explore three case studies – Janet Cardiff's sound walks (the first of which was created for Walkman performance) and two headphone theatre projects. Each of these examples addresses a question that Karen Collins has articulated in her examination of the video-game player – that is, 'How is interacting *with* sound different from listening *to* sound?' (2013: 23).

Case study: Janet Cardiff's sound walks

The first of Cardiff's audio projects, 'Forest Walk', was devised in 1991 while the artist was in residency at the Banff Centre in Canada – a spectacularly scenic location at high altitude in the Rocky Mountains. The twelve-minute performance invited the Walkman-wearing audience member to switch on the player while standing by the garbage can outside the Banff Centre's Walter Phillips Gallery and then to head out on a trail, identifiable by 'an eaten-out dead tree. Looks like ants' (Cardiff Miller – all quotations from the walks and from the artist come from this website). After delivering the walk's initial instructions, the voice ('Janet') periodically stops talking to be replaced by the sounds of footsteps, of a hand brushing tree bark, of crows cawing and of a train's horn in the distance. The effect of her sound score is to prompt the audience-participant to walk in step with both the speaker and what Schafer would call the hi-fi soundscape of a rural setting. Every now and then, 'Janet' shares her observations with us in a flat, somewhat affectless voice so that she veers between companion and guide: 'Walk up the path. I haven't been in this forest for a long time ... it's good to get away from the Centre, from building noises, to idyllic nature. Ok, there's a fork in the path, take the trail to the right.' It is almost as if the original audience for Cage's '4'33"' had been wrested from the concert hall into the soundscape of 'Forest Walk' to practice contextual listening in motion. Fundamental to Cardiff's audio performance is the participant's collaborative process with the artist, literally following in her footsteps, tuning the ear to the sounds Cardiff heard in the work's creation and collaborating in an act of acoustic world-making.

But, as the listener discovers, 'Forest Walk' is no rural idyll; no sooner is the ambulatory audience member immersed in the 'secret theatre' of Cardiff's Walkman environment than different voices interrupt the newly intimate connection with 'Janet'. Her friendly words are displaced by those of 'Jvox' and 'Man's Voice', rendered in an altogether different timbre:

Jvox I just want to be with you.

Man's Voice It's so beautiful in the forest at night .... It's kind of spooky though.

Jvox We've had wonderful times.

Man's Voice It's my fucked personality, blame it on me.

The lone audio-walker, by now some way into a forest of very large spruce and pine trees, suddenly finds herself in the role of unexpected and unsuspecting eavesdropper, obliged to listen in on another relationship between two people whose biographies are unknown. The couple's exchanges are part erotic, part angry, part terrified. The listener cannot help but look around: are these people here? Are they following me? Should I be scared? 'Forest Walk' intercuts the cliché of the bucolic mountain hike with nightmarish interior sequences that have no obvious place in the immediate sonic experience of the setting. The Walkman prosthetic provides no comfort or reassurance, just the imperative march of recorded footsteps and occasional instructions to continue the endeavour alongside 'Janet'. As Cardiff has explained, the 'virtual recorded soundscape has to mimic the real physical one in order to create a new world as a seamless combination of the two. My voice gives directions but also relates thoughts and narrative elements, which instils in the listener a desire to continue and finish the walk'. More accurately, this desire is fuelled by both pleasure (for the walk itself) and anxiety (prompted by the odd and disruptive interpolations of Jvox and Man). The impetus 'to finish the walk' suggests the terms of the contract between the sound recording and the participant. Without the listener, the performance does not happen; in other words, the listener's role is what sound artist Norie Neumark has described as 'co-compositional' (2017: 32).

The Walter Phillips Gallery at the Banff Centre reprised 'Forest Walk' in 2011, twenty years after its first creation, and it was more than a little revealing to find I had so forgotten 'the Walkman years' that I needed instructions on how to operate the device and, of course, the forest had grown and changed in the intervening decades, making getting lost an inevitability, however rigorously instructions were obeyed. The soundscape became, in its retrospective framing, more of an experience of the forest's ghosts – a distant but present sound archive. 'Forest Walk' in 2011 was, too, a record of the area's environmental shifts and changes, not the least of which was the exponential growth of tourism witnessed by the persistent interruption of tourists' voices drifting upward from a viewpoint not too far away. To encounter 'Forest Walk' belatedly invited a process of making and remaking the soundscape of the Walkman's 'secret theatre', exercised through the dispersed time frame of then and now. Of this first audio walk, Cardiff has since written:

> It didn't have very good instructions and the quality of my mixing was terrible since it was mixed on a 4-track cassette deck, but the work really inspired me and changed my thinking about art. Probably only 10 people heard it at the time, but it was the prototype for all the walks that followed. When I listen to it now, I can appreciate the freshness and looseness, even with all of the bad editing.

As Cardiff suggests, the 'Forest Walk' experiment established a performance practice that the artist has now developed in more than twenty other 'walks' for sites and events across the world. For these projects Cardiff now uses the technology of binaural recording which 'reproduces sound the way it is heard by human ears, as opposed to stereo recording, which does not take into account the distance between the ears and the "headspace" in the middle. Sounds are clearly located in a quasi-physical space, producing the seemingly naturalistic production of sound as experienced in the real world' (Klich 2017: 370). The advantage of binaural sound played back through headphones is, then, that the sound seems to come from the surrounding environment and not from the instrument itself.

Most of Cardiff's walks since the first in Banff have been commissioned by and designed for museums or galleries in urban settings. Some of them involve walks on city streets such as 'The Missing Voice: Case Study B' (1999), a performance that leads the participant from the Whitechapel Library to Liverpool Street Station in London; others explore interior spaces, such as 'The Telephone Call' (2001), the second of Cardiff's video walks. 'The Telephone Call' was staged at the San Francisco Museum of Modern Art (SFMoMA) for the '010101, Art in Technological Times' exhibition. This video walk asked the audience-participant to follow pre-recorded film on a small digital camera that was also equipped with headphones. The user saw a film of the museum space that they were in at that moment, 'live', and thus the performance had the participant move through identical actual and filmed environments and, as with the audio-only walks, follow sonic instructions. Cardiff notes: 'The architecture in the video stays the same as the physical world, but the people and their actions change, so there is a strange disjunction for the viewer about what is real.' The premise for 'The Telephone Call' came from the idea that visitors to museums and art galleries often construct biographies for and stories about the other people they see there and, sometimes, develop fantasies of chance meetings with these strangers.

Unlike the one-sided telephone 'conversation' in Cocteau's *The Human Voice*, Cardiff's piece allows participants to eavesdrop on both parties to the titular call. We hear a phone ringing and the sound of someone beside us taking their phone out of their bag:

Janet Hello,

Bernard What are you thinking about?

Janet Who is this?

Bernard What do you mean? I'm sitting right beside you.

Janet We have to go now. Point the camera where I'm pointing it. Synchronize your movements with mine. Stand up. Walk to the right. Follow this woman. Go behind the stairs. Now walk past her.

Like the earlier 'Forest Walk', 'The Telephone Call' trades on the uncanny, deploying voice and sound effects to produce and pump up anxiety in the body of the listener. The audience-participant is hailed as Janet's collaborator ('Synchronize your movements with mine') but never has quite enough information from her to know exactly how they should participate in her scene and to what purpose(s).

Without any predictable sense of what comes next, participants in 'The Telephone Call' found themselves more and more conscious of their own affective responses to the increasingly confusing performance script. John S. Weber, the show's curator at SFMoMA, suggested that 'listening to Cardiff's voice, people are suspended between Janet's invented world and the real world' (Cardiff Miller). The walk ends with Janet curtly saying 'Goodbye', that conventional farewell of an everyday phone call, yet participants were often uncertain, Weber noted, 'as to whether the piece was in fact really over when the video stopped. They described thinking and hoping that everyone around them – who had, of course, just been absorbed into Cardiff's theater – might still have lines to speak and roles to play' (Cardiff Miller). The curator also observed that audience-participants consistently described their experience of 'The Telephone Call' 'in virtually sexual terms: the mingling of bodies, the feeling of being "in" someone and having someone inside them; a sense of unusually close physical communion with another person. A number of visitors observed that they needed to cry in the elevator after finishing the piece' (Cardiff Miller). This anecdote marks a fundamental difference between reception of *The Human Voice* in a conventional theatre setting, where the audience is obviously outside the acoustic world of the stage, and Cardiff's audio/video installations, where the audience is required to inhabit and move through the soundscape as much an actor in the work as Cardiff's fictional speakers.

Writing about his experience of participating in 'The Telephone Call', Peter Salvatore Petralia described the anxiety as 'tangible', but he also suggested that the most powerful part for him was 'the fascinating layering of real and recorded time that the headphone format created' (2014: 96). His reaction reminds us, then, that while headphone theatre puts a premium on sound (in both its production and reception elements), the genre can also be an effective dramaturgical tool for explorations of and challenges to theatrical time and space.

Listening to women: Andrea Hornick and Luce Irigaray

It is little wonder that Cardiff's audio- and video walks have been commonly staged in museum settings since these cultural institutions had been particularly quick to adopt the new mobile audio technology that the Walkman and its competitor devices offered. Since the 1980s, audio guides have become omnipresent in museum and gallery settings and are designed to offer their users, typically at extra cost, an informed viewing of the materials on display. The British Museum, for example, advertises its guide as providing '260 expert commentaries on highlight objects' as well as offering the chance to create 'a digital souvenir you can send to yourself with a list of what you visited' (British Museum). In other words, the contract between the sound performance and the listener is one that accepts the museum's construction of what is important ('highlight objects'), what a visitor should want to know to enhance their understanding ('expert commentaries') and what that visitor could retain or archive ('a digital souvenir' – a value-added benefit that enacts, to evoke Jonathan Sterne's concept, a 'resonant tomb' of touristic experience). The composition and distribution of these audio guides exemplify the soft power of museums, stratified and organized by way of a Deleuzean territorialization of its collection- and visitor-subjects. Like any authoritative practice, however, the audio guide is ripe for appropriation and remediation, subsequent acts of deterritorialization that might strive to undo the structured pathways of museum organization and to liberate the visitor to receive – and produce – contradictory narratives and competing fields of knowledge.

Revisionist audio guide ably describes Andrea Hornick's *Unbounded Histories* (2017), commissioned by the Barnes Foundation in Philadelphia. This museum is best known for its extensive holdings of French impressionist and post-impressionist paintings (including almost 200 Renoirs – more than any other collection in the world), but its founder Albert C. Barnes (1872–1951) collected widely and far beyond his French favourites. Indeed, the collection houses 2,500 items that encompass visual art, artefacts and furniture from all periods and cultures – a remarkable and unique diversity that Barnes himself painstakingly organized in a series of small rooms. Almost every available inch of wall space in each and every room is packed with art and objects, arranged to deliberately mix periods, styles and countries of origin. Barnes's meticulous curatorial practice also insisted on withholding the usual descriptive information labels posted by each work of art; instead there are pictorial guide sheets available in each room for those visitors who are determined to know the provenance of an item. Moreover, his bequest insisted on the maintenance in perpetuity of the rooms and their contents as he had arranged them. By conventional standards of museum management, then, the Barnes Foundation is wildly different yet extraordinarily rigid. *Unbounded Histories*, as its title signals, looked to pry loose the visitor's experience of the collection through Hornick's sound play on and critique of the genre of the audio guide. Her soundtrack was available for streaming, without cost, to any visitor with a web-enabled phone. If needed, headphones could be borrowed from the Barnes Foundation.

Hornick's process for the creation of *Unbounded Histories* started with sound experimentation. Over a period of weeks, she visited the collection after hours, sometimes with invited guests, and created thirty 'drum journeys' – shamanic drumming rituals where she asked her spirit animal to show her how the objects in a room were connected and how they might be transformed: 'I asked how this information was relevant to myself and anyone who would listen to the narratives generated from shamanic vision that were conflated with the accepted art histories in the resulting epic poem sound work, *Unbounded Histories*' (Hornick). The result was an emphatically feminist re-imagination of the collection that offered its listening audience an alternative route, literally and metaphorically, through the many rooms that Albert Barnes organized and oversaw.

Like Cardiff's, Hornick's voice is deliberately affectless (curator Martha Lucy described it as 'robotic'). Distinctively, the artist deployed a kind of staccato delivery – a stark contrast to the confident authority that typifies modes of speaking in a more usual museum audio guide. Navigating what is unquestionably a perverse history of the collection – it lived up to its titular adjective 'unbounded' – the audience-participant was frequently incorporated into Hornick's creative act: for example, in Room 2, the listener was told to pay attention to a vase of flowers in one of the paintings and that this bouquet would be your contribution to a dinner; later, in Room 13, the listener was invited to the dinner pictured in another artwork where Hornick indicated we will be served a *bouillabaisse* that has taken three days to prepare. The listener was reminded then, too, to bring something for the table (presumably the flowers?). Elsewhere, our guide's reading of Renoir's famous 'Bois de la Chaise (Noirmoutier)' (1892) commented not on the conventional aspects of art criticism that a conventional audio guide would celebrate (colour palette, brush stroke, depth of image, historical precedents, provenance and acquisition history) but instead merely pointed out the appearance of the two women pictured in the landscape, 'Attire: seaside casual for a late spring early evening gathering'. Other interpolations in Hornick's guide suggested illicit sexual relationships between subjects who not only occupied different paintings but were also found in different rooms – a fantasy of after-hours shenanigans in the museum collection that tapped into familiarity with the popular *Night at the Museum* film trilogy.

Throughout the 'tour', Hornick's conversation with the audience-participant was replete with both intimate and everyday details. Her objective was to invoke listeners to hear – and thus see – extraordinarily famous artworks anew: she dwelt on the minutiae of domestic life and the texture of interpersonal relationships within a single work or between several of them. The speaker was determined to thwart any expectation that the guide would deliver expert opinion on the exceptional talent of the artists and instead challenged her audience to be active participants in making art history rather than performing as its passive receiver. The audio walk started on the gallery's mezzanine level where the audience-participant was instructed to kneel in front of a statue of the Virgin Mary 'who is looking benevolently down toward you to reassure' (in other words, the audio walk recognized at its inception the audience's inherent performance anxiety). The narrator-guide pointed out the encounter in this space takes place between women from three different 'belief systems' – Mary holding Christ, a ninth-century French fertility bust and a Spiderwoman-motif blanket woven by Navajo 'women sitting on Mother Earth'

(Barnes). Thus *Unbounded Histories* implicated the listener in a performance that refused the authority of the audio guide, creating an exemplary act of Deleuzean deterritorialization in its rejection of the lines of flight of 'expert' interpretation. Hornick's work at the Barnes made a sonic contribution to the very many historiographical projects of recovery and revision for all genres of women's cultural production that feminist scholars have undertaken since the 1960s.

Attentive readers of *Sound* will have noticed that the first examples of 'experiential sound' are also the first appearances of women in this book. Their projects draw attention to the fact that Sections One and Two featured only men thinking about and making sound, a fact underscored by my intermittent additions of '[sic]' to annotate use of the 'universal' he in so many of the quotations from classical and avant-garde sound theorists. As well, theories of listening complied with the same universal assumption – that the listener was a man. That the work of women in the sonic domain emerges only late in the twentieth century speaks volumes as to the gendered performance of and scholarly interest in sound. 'Thinking historically about gendered soundscapes', Christine Ehrick writes, 'can help us conceptualize sound as a space where categories of "male" and "female" are constituted' (Ehrick 2015). She rightly argues that we urgently tune in to sound as a signifier of power. In this context of theory for theatre studies, it is worth remembering, too, that a study of the top 10 subsidized theatres in the UK (conducted by Elizabeth Freestone of Pentabus Theatre in conjunction with the *Guardian* newspaper) found, in 2011–12, only 6.6 per cent of all sound designers employed were women and that six of those ten theatres had 'no female sound designers at all employed as part of their creative teams' (Cabanas 2013).

Notwithstanding the long gendered history of sound, it is evident that an immediate consequence of new sound technologies that were relatively inexpensive, accessible and thoroughly mobile was to open up the field of sound production to women artists. Even if many theorists have continued to assume a 'universal' – which is to say, man's – perspective (the narcissistic mastery of Schafer's headphone listening, for example), many experiential sound projects press us to consider matters of difference and obligations of ethical practice as fundamental to making and understanding acoustic environments. This task could not be better captured than in the opening sentence of French feminist theorist Luce Irigaray's proposal for ethical listening: 'Let us begin with: how am I to listen to you?' (1996: 115).

Irigaray's meditation on listening offers that 'I am listening to you as someone and something I do not know yet, on the basis of a freedom and an openness put aside for this moment. I am listening to you: I encourage something unexpected to emerge, some becoming' (1996: 116–17). As the antithesis of an always already territorialized act of listening, ethical auditory practice attends above all to the position of the other: 'Listening to you requires that I make myself available, that I be once more and always capable of silence' (Irigaray 1996: 118). In the promise to 'make myself available', I hear an openness beyond the specific of the ear – rather, that the undertaking she imagines is fully embodied. This is an idea that resonates with Gillian Siddall and Ellen Waterman's proposition of 'sounding the body'. They insist, rightly, that sound is a physical phenomenon: 'Sound is active: it travels, insinuates, reverberates, repeats, and fades away. Sound is sensual: it whispers and shouts, tickles your ear, and thumps in your chest. We embody, and are embodied through, sound' (2016: 2). Thinking through improvised sound practices that take place on gendered, sexed, raced, classed, disabled and technologized bodies, they argue that these practices make 'negotiations of (material and discursive) subjectivity audible' (2016: 3). Rather than thinking about sound as a discrete category within theatrical performance, then, we are challenged to understand it multi-modally and interactively.

Affective theatres of embodied sound

While the innovation of Walkman technology literally allowed for the development of a new performance genre (the audio-/video walk), the evolution of wireless sound technology has been a boon to a broader range of theatrical work. The invention in 1994 of Bluetooth by Dutch engineer Jaap Haartsen and its application in wireless communication between a mobile phone and a hands-free headset set in motion the possibilities of headphone theatre. The two case studies examined in this section take up quite different topics (brain injury, global arms trade) but both performances deploy headphones to create what Hosokawa called a *mise en oeuvre* in the body.

Shannon Yee's *Reassembled, Slightly Askew* (2015) and Rimini Protokoll's *Situation Rooms* (2013) require their audiences to wear headphones that relay oral histories to evoke bodily responses generated by the act of listening. These two works are exemplary test cases, through the expectation of the audience's participatory role, for Irigaray's question: 'how am I to listen to you?' Intended, then, to inspire ethical listening, *Reassembled* and *Situation Rooms* deliver oral histories of their subjects to the listeners' headsets. As a historiographical method, the collection of oral histories has challenged the composition of traditional history-making and, at the same time, been an important strategy in recording the experiences of peoples who have otherwise been absent from that history. As Patricia Leavy suggests, oral history has been crucial as 'a way of accessing subjugated voices' (2011: 5). *Reassembled* and *Situation Rooms* are invested in having 'subjugated voices' heard and, moreover, both structure their sonic texts to work with and respect the practices of this methodology:

> Ontologically, oral history is based on a conception of research as a *process*, not an event. The practice of oral

history assumes that meaning isn't 'waiting out there' to be discovered, but rather that meaning is generated during the research process. (Leavy 2011: 7)

In other words, the audience receives the histories aurally but the performance requires their listening participation to create meaning. Like Cardiff's walks, these performances are co-compositional.

Case study: Shannon Yee's *Reassembled, Slightly Askew*

Reassembled, Slightly Askew is a ninety-minute, immersive headphone performance that tells the story of Belfast artist Shannon Yee's falling gravely ill with a rare brain infection, her subsequent experience of a medically induced coma and multiple neurosurgeries and the impact of the long, slow process of rehabilitation with 'an acquired brain injury' (*Reassembled*). It invites the listener to encounter a sonic interrogation of Yee's brain illness and injury – an acoustic experience of the traumatized body. The performance takes the form of an interactive soundscape that asks listeners to experience Yee's medical history sonically and to occupy that narrative ethically, affectively and, above all, compassionately.

Reassembled was co-created over a five-year period with an interdisciplinary team of artists: playwright Yee worked with a director, a sound artist, a choreographer and a dramaturg as well as in collaboration with the neurosurgeon and head injury liaison nurse who oversaw Yee's treatment and recovery. Initially she had considered the possibility of making a radio play about her experiences in hospital and met with Anna Newell (who would later become *Reassembled*'s director) to explore working in this genre. Yee had conceived of a radio play since she was still struggling with visual perception and Newell recommended that they work with Paul Stapleton, based at Queen's University Belfast, because of his interest in site-specific sound creation using binaural technology. After the five years of collaborative development, *Reassembled, Slightly Askew* had its first performances in 2015 and since that time has toured in the UK, Ireland and Canada.

As part of the 2018 programming for Calgary's High Performance Rodeo festival, *Reassembled* was staged at the St. Louis Hotel – a 1914 building no longer serving its original purpose but conserved as one of the city's heritage sites and now chiefly occupied by offices. Ticket holders were instructed to arrive at least thirty minutes before the advertised start time and were asked to complete 'admission forms', providing generalized demographic information and requiring a sign-off on several warning clauses. All belongings (wallets, phones, coats, shoes) were left in care of the 'hospital reception'. Steven, *Reassembled*'s only live actor, attached a plastic hospital bracelet to the wrist of each participant as we waited in the building foyer for an available bed. The high-ceilinged main room of the hotel's ground floor was transformed into a hospital ward for the performance: neat rows of narrow hospital beds, each immaculately made with white sheets (showing off properly tight 'hospital corners') and a white-cased pillow. Small metal tables stood at the sides of the beds. Each performance member was directed to a bed and instructed to lie and wait for the 'nurse' to fit headsets and an eye mask. We were told to raise a hand if we had any concerns or problems during the performance, and we would be assisted in leaving the room.

Crucial to the performance of *Reassembled, Slightly Askew* were its sensory parameters: stillness, darkness and sound. The narrowness of the bed meant that lying more or less motionless on one's back was the only viable option and the blackout eye mask effectively eliminated any light. Even before the soundtrack began, the performance experience was unavoidably sonic. Deprived of sight and movement, the immediate environment comprised only the faint murmurs of the nurse as he equipped other participants one-by-one and the sound of one's own breathing. I thought of Beckett's 'Breath', at least until the show proper began.

Yee's story – unlike Beckett's – is expressed as a totally interior experience, both for her as the speaker and for the listener through the headphone delivery and in the focus created by the absence of other sensory stimuli:

> The audio technology makes the sound three-dimensional, causing listeners to feel they are inside Shannon's head, viscerally experiencing her descent into coma, brain surgeries, early days in the hospital, and re-integration into the world with a hidden disability. It is a new kind of storytelling, never done before about this topic, that places the listener safely in the first-person perspective to increase empathy and understanding – it's one step better than walking in someone's shoes, it's living in someone else's head. (*Reassembled*)

Yee is an able storyteller, but her narrative is only part of what we hear. 'Living in someone else's head' involves listening to the experiences she endured: doctors and nurses, her partner and family members all talking to her at different stages of the illness, coma and recovery. We not only eavesdrop on questions that repeat over and again, both as part of medical monitoring and as expressions of concern from understandably terrified loved ones, but also find ourselves empathizing with Yee's frustrations in not being able to respond or intervene. Her enforced silence is replicated in our bodies as we listen to her story.

This is what happened to Yee: in December 2008, she was admitted to the acute Neurosurgical Ward of Belfast's Royal Victoria Hospital, only later to discover that she was likely no more than one hour away from death from a subdural empyema. We listen in on her experience of a craniotomy that involved, among other things, the removal of a bone flap from her skull that was then stored in a subcutaneous pouch in her abdomen for safekeeping. A few weeks later she has a second neurosurgery. *Reassembled*'s soundtrack often concentrates on Yee's attempts to forge some logic from what seemed to her at the time so illogical and bizarre. She shares the raw distress of her situation, especially in failure after failure to communicate successfully with others and in her crushing frustration with the process of learning to walk again. The most mundane medical intervention becomes a sound site of trauma evidenced, for example, by the dread that Yee's voice conveys when medical technicians arrived for what seemed like the millionth time to take yet more blood from unwilling veins. My listening body tensed up every time a technician approached Yee with a needle and responded with involuntary shivers in the hearing of Yee's fragmented thoughts as her brain surgeries were conducted. These events offer the audience plenty of proof for the vividness of the sonic imagination. They also remind us of the common injunction that we should 'listen to our bodies' as part of self-care (Rice 2015: 100).

Lyn Gardner, in her review of the show's performance at the Battersea Arts Centre (London), describes her listening act as the sensation of 'experiencing the world from underwater, or via a patchy radio signal' (2016). The dislocation and disruption in hearing that the sonic environment of *Reassembled* realizes is an effect, of course, of the use of binaural recording – a technique that, as Klich notes, produces 'an aesthetic of digital simulation, setting up an encounter for the audience with a sonic virtual reality that emphasises corporeal sensation, affect, and embodiment' (2017: 366). I was surprised and occasionally a little overcome by the intensity of the whole body experience that *Reassembled* stimulated, although that same intensity (the need, and desire, to pay close attention) overrode my usual tendency towards extreme squeamishness in the face of any medical information or representation. In all honesty, I had not expected to make it to the end of the performance, but I did. And I was content to lie in silence for several minutes at the end of the show, even after 'the nurse' had collected the headphones and eye mask. Was that continued stillness and quiet part of the performance? Was my self-inflicted silence a necessary re-integration into a world where movement and light had returned? How do we, as listening subjects for headphone theatre, move from a single mode of encounter – sound – to a multi-modal negotiation of the performance space? And how does Yee's soundscape, her memories, transfer to our own? Chris Wenn proposes that the very design of headphones intends to create 'a "pure" listening experience' and observes that 'sound does not linger within the acoustic space inhabited by the listener; its sensory capture in the memory of the listener is the only existence it has' (2015: 244). (Wenn's essay on headphone listening describes his own sound design for a performance of Lachlan Philpott's *The Trouble with Harry*, staged at the Melbourne Festival, and is an excellent bridge between theoretical concepts and practical strategies.)

The freakishness and severity of what happened to Yee – a woman of barely thirty, an illness that started with a sinus infection and almost caused death, demanded extraordinary determination to recover from partial paralysis and challenged her with the re-learning of simple everyday tasks – required of its audience an aghast attentiveness, the attempt to experience headphone listening as the conduit to getting inside Yee's head. Her sounding body was rendered as the audience's acoustical theatre, to be viscerally experienced and ethically heard. Binaural sound technology is what makes this relationship possible and, in this context, Klich's analysis of its production-reception structure is helpful. She explains that the technology creates an 'environment [that] unfolds around the individual audience member as a sonically rendered narrative or sonic-scenic poem, with a dramaturgy that is reliant on the audience's intersensorial processing of the mediated score' (2017: 368). The provision of an aftershow to *Reassembled* suggested that Yee and her collaborators wanted the opportunity to debrief their audiences on their experience of this 'intersensorial processing'.

Ahead of the performance, audience members had been invited to stay and watch 'Behind the Story', a twenty-fiveminute video documentary about the interdisciplinary creation process for *Reassembled*. This was, Steven assured us, an optional extra and if we didn't want to attend the screening, we could sign up for a link to the documentary on the company's YouTube channel that would be emailed to us at a later date (a link to 'Behind the Story' is available on the Companion Website for this book). On the night I saw *Reassembled*, only some of the audience, perhaps five or six people, moved to another room to view the company's documentary; I chose to sign up for the emailed link, mostly because I wanted to take time to see how the inside of Yee's head stayed, as it were, in the inside of my own, to think through the sensory impact of her experiential body on mine.

Beyond its theatrical tours, *Reassembled* has also been performed for professional audiences such as the British Association of Neuroscience Nurses and delivered as a component of medical training. In 'Behind the Story', Yee's neurosurgeon expresses some initial scepticism about the utility and relevance of creative examinations of illness but confesses that *Reassembled*'s first-person perspective gave him and his team access to information that he could not have acquired any other way. This was a provocative example that suggested possibilities for pedagogically based and therapeutic theatre practices to work more specifically with 'sounding the body' to address specific social, medical and educational issues.

While Yee's drama worked to restrict the audience-participant by inhibiting motion and removing light, the next case study – of Rimini Protokoll's *Situation Rooms* – explores how sound delivered via headphones works as a prompt for participatory action on the part of the audience.

Case study: Rimini Protokoll's *Situation Rooms*

Helgard Kim Haug, Stefan Kaegi and Daniel Wetzel are a team of author-directors who have worked together since 2000. They took the name Rimini Protokoll some two years later and since 2003 have been based in Berlin. Their *Situation Rooms* was first performed at the Ruhrtriennale (Germany) in 2013, and this performance has toured internationally in the years that followed. A fully participatory experience, *Situation Rooms* is driven by sound-based autobiographical narratives that foster in its audiences the active examination of both individual and large-scale political ethics in a globalized theatre of war.

Described by the company as a 'multi-player video piece', creators Haug, Kaegi and Wetzel have also adapted the audio component of the performance as a radio play for public broadcaster WDR (West German Broadcasting Cologne).

The starting point for the project's development had been a striking image from a real-life theatre of war: the photograph seen across the globe of President Obama, Hillary Clinton (then serving as Secretary of State) and other members of the Obama Administration crowded into the White House Situation Room where, on 1 May 2011, they watched the live performance of 'Operation Neptune's Spear', an action that would culminate in the assassination by US Navy SEALs of a sleeping Osama bin Laden. The photograph's stage was one of the most iconic centres of global power, and the image was surely captured with a worldwide audience in mind. But, as a photograph, it epitomizes familiar ocular-centrist interpretation. *Situation Rooms* set out, then, to deconstruct the authority created and disseminated by this single-perspective and aesthetically impressive portrait. To this end, the Rimini Protokoll team researched the global arms trade and collected the real-life stories of twenty people whose lives had been shaped by and/or entangled in this industry. The first-person autobiographical narratives of these twenty found subjects informed the audio track of *Situation Rooms*. Some of the occupations represented in these stories are predictable, given the subject matter – a drone pilot, a weapons expert, a human rights lawyer and a child soldier; others less so perhaps – a computer hacker, a surgeon for Doctors Without Borders, a cafeteria manager at a Russian arms factory.

Audience-participants for *Situation Rooms* receive an iPad mini and Bluetooth headphones to equip them for a multi-continental journey through a network of fifteen scenes in rooms linked by doors, elevators, stairs and corridors. Twenty audience-participants are admitted for each performance. Like the digital camera used in Cardiff's video walks, the iPad of *Situation Rooms* contained filmed scenes in each of the rooms the participant might visit. Each tablet housed a selection of ten stories from the available twenty (these are pre-loaded and organized without an overarching explanation or a capacity for the participant to intervene in either the selection or the order in which the specific vignettes are engaged). In the cramped spaces of the 'situation rooms', each participant must perform tasks described in the first-person narratives and follow instructions that require fast-paced movement in and between the various locales. In short, the audience member's task is to convert hearing into acting. This is what Karen Collins, in her theory of video-game playing, would call 'kinesonic synchresis' – the fusion of sounds with actions (2013: 32). In describing *Situation Rooms* as a 'multi-player video piece', creators Haug, Kaegi and Wetzel acknowledge the influence of and alignment with gaming and draw on the likelihood of their audiences' familiarity with the genre as players.

The geo-political contexts of the individual scenes that comprise *Situation Rooms* are remarkably diverse: they range from a weapons fair in Abu Dhabi to a schoolroom in the South Sudan via a conference room in Paris. Throughout the seventy minutes of the performance, participants are given orders to 'perform' for the people whose stories they have been assigned, and they must exercise careful listening skills to stay on track and fully comprehending of what's required in and between individual scenes. Sometimes a participant might criss-cross a single situation room so that she hears and plays different roles and perspectives within that one setting. In other words, *Situation Rooms* works best when participants demonstrate a proficiency in kinesonic synchresis – drawing on a repertoire of practices familiar from well-rehearsed habits and skills in video-game playing. The show's objective, as Nikolaus Hirsch writes in the curatorial essay to the *Situation Rooms* text, is to avoid any obvious moralizing about the arms trade: 'Rimini

Protokoll shows that "for" and "against" isn't quite so simple, but that increasingly the terrain of ethics itself is a minefield' (15). (All quotations from Hirsch's essay and the audio script are taken from the *Situation Rooms* text sold by the company at their performances.)

I participated in *Situation Rooms* when it was programmed as part of the 2016 Luminato Festival in Toronto. These performances took place at the Hearn Generating Station, a vast, decommissioned power plant some distance from downtown (a shuttle bus took audiences at regularly scheduled times from the city centre to the Port Lands area, a brownfield industrial site). The space was dark, dank and isolated – cold rather than inviting and amply populated by Luminato volunteers who made sure that no visitor strayed into off-limits areas of the Hearn. The exterior of multi-room structure built for *Situation Rooms* revealed nothing to a pre-performance gaze: it appeared to be a large plain box with a selection of doors, each bearing a different number. All belongings had to be divested ahead of the performance (deposited into secure lockers), effectively triangulating the individual body with its technological prosthetic eyes and ears (the iPad and the headphones).

When ticket holders were told to begin, the first audio instruction required each participant to enter the space through a specifically numbered door and from that moment, *Situation Rooms* becomes a personal, sonically driven engagement with the ten people you 'meet'. Of course, as a participant, you regularly stumble into (and sometimes over) the other nineteen people taking part in that performance time slot. The intense concentration required to process the density of information from the audio track distracted from normal patterns of spatial management with participants frequently bumping into walls and into each other. Sometimes instructions involved watching another participant perform an action, only to find oneself in that role and repeating it a few minutes later. As Vicky Frost wrote of her experience participating in *Situation Rooms* at the Perth Festival, 'for more than an hour you are so busy living this piece of extraordinary art that that you do really become it' (2014) – a sense of the migration through the performance from hearing-acting (kinesonic synchresis) to becoming the other.

Like Shannon Yee's *Reassembled*, this project laminates another's first-person perspective onto the participant's body through sound. The parameters of each story heard inform the actions the participant undertakes. We only listen and never speak: we cannot converse with the people whose lives we perform nor do we engage with our fellow performers. Sometimes, two or more participants are co-performers in a single scene, but we only hear our individual 'lines' in the headset. Yet, in principle at least, participants act out the idea that openness to the other requires a making available of oneself: a performance of passive listening but requiring active embodiment and the goal of ethical becoming. In the programme for the Toronto performances, Jutta Brendemühl (programme director at the city's Goethe Institut) described her response to *Situation Rooms*:

> The piece has not left me to this day. I remember holding my tablet, unsure how to navigate the huge container we entered, how to react to shifting situation rooms with their respective stories and cast of characters, how to move with the other participants in communal silence while interrupted by gun shots over my headphones. (I flinched or ducked more than once)

One of my most vivid experiences in the *Situation Rooms* was, in tandem with Brendemühl's recollection, the sound of gunfire – extreme and terrifying noise that could destroy any pretence of safety in a split second. I suspect that this sound cue stays so emphatically with those of us who never hear gunshots as part of our day-to-day lives and because of its involuntary translation into bodily response ('I flinched or ducked'). Among the ten stories I was assigned was that of 'the Marksman', a German police officer named Andreas Geikowski. In this scene the participant enters a room set up as a shooting range, listening first to Geikowski describing in detail the gun he owned for sports (he has been world champion more than once in 'dynamic high caliber shooting' [24]). But the description of Geikowski's passion for sport shooting soon migrated into an instruction to perform:

> I assume that you've never fired a gun? To shoot, stand with your legs spread, a bit wider than your shoulders. Pick up the weapon with your strong hand, which is usually the right. Now check if the weapon is loaded. To do this, pull this lever forward and swing the barrel out. The strength comes only from your lower arms. (23)

His monologue continued, detail after detail, until the command to 'pull the trigger slowly backward until it shoots' (24). I have no interest in ever firing a gun but his instructions felt coercive and I hesitated at 'failing' the performance. Was this an effective strategy to have me listen to, and then embody, a different perspective than my own? To act out something I would avoid at all costs in real life? The company suggests that *Situation Rooms* 'offers the listener the chance to adopt the different positions as if they were character masks, trying them on and seeing how it feels to be inside a particular individual's skin and inside their logic' (Rimini). I don't doubt the affective power of character masks and the efficacy of a crafted soundscape as a prompt to learn through action, but the tension I felt in whether or not to do Geikowski's bidding was every bit as powerful as the anxiety I felt for Yee when she struggled to communicate at all as she emerged from a medically induced coma. And, like Cardiff's audio- and video walks, *Situation Rooms* relies upon sound to create and maintain a condition of anxiety in the listener.

Since I have made the claim for 'experiential sound' as a watershed moment – marking the entry, finally, of women's voices into this study of the theories of theatrical sound – I think it is important to record the role of women's voices in the headphone theatre of *Situation Rooms*. Of the twenty perspectives available to audience-participants, only three are women's: Barbara Happe, a German environmental and human rights activist; Irina Panibratowa, a Russian 'nutritional engineer' who worked for more than a decade in the cafeterias of a weapons factory near Perm before leaving Russia to live in Germany; and Aziza, the wife and mother in 'Family R', a family of five, refugees from war and other dangers, who had eventually settled in Germany. It is perhaps not unexpected that a performance about the global arms industry would be primarily a drama about men, but the 'terrain of ethics', to use Hirsch's phrase, was a minefield strewn with gendered decisions for the participant.

Among the few women's voices in *Situation Rooms*, I encountered only Aziza (she shared with her husband the narrative of 'Family R'). The couple were born in Darfur but both had left to study in Libya where they had well-paid jobs and comfortable professional lives. When rumours spread that all Sudanese in Libya were in fact mercenaries working for Colonel Gadaffi's regime, Aziza and Rushwan fled the country in a boat and spent the next eight months in a refugee camp in Italy before getting themselves and their three children to Germany. Their story is narrated, in a matter-of-fact style, in a room that represents their apartment home: Aziza speaks from her place seated on the room's sofa (the same one, except empty, that the participant is instructed to face while listening). Her backstory reminds the participant that behind the appearance of an ordinary domestic life, there can be an exceptional history that requires our willingness to hear ('Listening to you requires that I make myself available', in Irigaray's words). But *Situation Rooms* allowed no time or space for reflection within the performance event. Where *Reassembled* stage managed conditions of reception to afford the primacy of the ear (no external distractions to mediate the injunction to get inside Yee's head), *Situation Rooms* drives the action by ear but requires the participant to keep moving as she hears. As participant-performer, I juggled many external distractions, often in the actions that must be completed, that undermine the authority of the spoken texts.

Ten oral histories disseminated in little more than an hour speaks to the company's goal of insisting participants engage many different points of view and, at the same time, recognize that an action in one part of the world can have devastating effects on lives elsewhere. The simple mathematics of time allocation dictated that these stories inevitably resembled the sound-bite documentaries typical to nightly news programming rather than an immersive learning opportunity. Without the opportunity for reflection, the scenarios seemed over-determined and mostly hopeless. In a reaction much like my own, Frost summarized her experience: 'I wondered at times whether the balance between interactivity and storytelling was a bit out; the impact of these important stories reduced because one is given so little time to really consider them. They become another element in the experience, rather than the driving force behind it' (2014). Nonetheless, the soundscape of *Situation Rooms* is premised on the value of oral histories enacted by others. The juxtaposition of stories from those accustomed to power and authority with those whose lives have been subject to and subjugated by the arms industry builds a performance environment that seeks an ethical listening practice. As Leavy notes, '[O]ral history connects biographical experience with the social/historical context in which biographies are played out. In other words, oral history allows researchers to make links between micro-level experiences and macro-level environments that shape and contain those experiences' (2011: 16). In *Situation Rooms*, the twenty participants act out those links to translate the sonic script into embodied performance.

Experiential sound is thoroughly theatrical in both its production and reception; it has expanded both theory and practices into more participatory, inclusive and democratized modes. Janet Cardiff's early adoption of personal sound technology (the Walkman) opened up performance installation to a new kind of mobility and to the enabling of the audience as co-creator/participant – and to do so not particularly or necessarily collectively but from the perspective of private space: a 'secret theatre' between her and her listener. The other examples in this section all explore the authority of history. Andrea Hornick's appropriation of the museum audio guide undermines both the institution's control of the critical narrative and visitors' assumptions about the production of interpretation and their own place outside it. *Reassembled* and *Situation Rooms* show the potential of oral histories to teach. All of these examples suggest how 'headphone theatre' exploits the private space of the audience-participant's ear and how that particular condition of reception almost inevitably encourages affective responses on the 'sounding body'.

Michael Bull has suggested that headphones transform 'the users' relationship to the environment' (2013a: 529) and while contemporary performances such as *Reassembled, Slightly Askew* and *Situation Rooms* utilize headset delivery to bring oral histories to life in audiences' experience of them, the impact of Bluetooth technology extends well beyond projects that seek to create and inform politically and ethically nuanced listeners. Think here of the enormously popular genre of 'Silent Disco', a performance practice where the body signals the sounds that individual listeners hear. The pleasure of headphones in a crowd, Wenn suggests, derives from the fact 'we are each individually in control yet in uncontrolled space' (2015: 247), a reminder, again, of how sound can reconfigure the spatialities of performance and of bodies in performance.

But despite what might be seen as value-added elements for a theatrical soundscape, these examples provide yet more evidence that modes of sonic performance and the theories of sound through which they might be understood remain resolutely Western. Cardiff's walks, Yee's *Reassembled* and Rimini Protokoll's *Situation Rooms* have all found enthusiastic audiences internationally, but almost exclusively in English-speaking and continental European countries. The proliferation and popularity of 'experiential sound' theatres begs the question as to how might we engage with performance soundscapes created in other places in the world and by artists for whom there may well be different and contradictory cultural histories of sound and practices of sound technologies? How would the theories reviewed in this book work to explicate other orders of cultural expression and, moreover, to promote different ways of thinking about the dramatic potentials of sound? Asian theatres, indigenous practices in Australasia and North America, religious rituals across Latin America – all of these performance forms, among many others, would challenge the ideas the Western narrative has developed.

Coda: Sound across the world

If scholars in theatre and performance studies have been virtually silent on the subject of non-Western sound, it is true, too, that other disciplines offer us few pathways to follow. The field-defining anthologies of Sound Studies – the *Oxford Handbook of Sound Studies*, Routledge's *The Sound Studies Reader*, the four volumes of *Sound Studies* – turn only very rarely to non-Western topics (the *Oxford Handbook* not at all) and, in step with much theatre and performance studies writing, typically limit discussion to specific case studies conducted in a single locality. *The Sound Studies Reader* is perhaps the most diverse: three contributions, among the book's total of forty-five, look at 'the voice of Algeria' (Frantz Fanon's 1965 essay), Islamic revival in Cairo and 'the aural public sphere' in Latin America, respectively. The lack of any expansive knowledge base for non-Western sonic traditions suggests that there is much work to do in order to address the methodological problem of opening up our disciplinary practice to pay more attention to the production of sound across the globe and to do so with a mindfulness towards ethical listening.

A rare prolegomenon to the study of sound worldwide can be found in the review essay 'Soundscapes: Towards a Sounded Anthropology' where the authors begin by suggesting that it is time to resituate recording technologies from the place of tool into a subject of scholarly interrogation:

> How might the discipline of anthropology develop if its practitioners stopped thinking of the field recording only as a source of data for the written work that then ensues and rather thought of the recording itself as a meaningful form? What if discussions of recording moved beyond inquiries about the state of the art in recording technology to how best to present and represent the sonorous enculturated worlds inhabited by people? (Samuels et al. 2010: 330)

In the absence of widely available performance histories for 'sonorous enculturated worlds' beyond the West, it is useful, at least, to think at least of those places where we have been encouraged to hear 'foreign' sound – that is, in the global circulation of intercultural performance.

In this context, Marcus Cheng Chye Tan has looked specifically at 'acoustic interculturalism', an articulation of 'the performative function of sound and music in intercultural performance' (2012: 21). His case studies – examinations of dramatic works by Ariane Mnouchkine, Yukio Ninagawa and Ong Keng Sen – elaborate how 'sound works to interrogate cultural boundaries' (2012: 49) and Tan suggests that these intercultural theatres challenge received expectations for auditory reception. He suggests that 'what is communicated becomes less certain and the "meanings" of such an aural experience become complicated and bewildering' (2012: 49). We might look here at one of Mnouchkine's best-known works *Les Atrides* (a four-play, ten-hour performance cycle where Euripides' *Iphigenie at Aulis* precedes Aeschylus's *Oresteia*) for which the production's composer, Jean Jacques Lemetre, provided a soundscape. Lemetre's music for the adapted Greek dramas was delivered in performance from 'a rustic bandstand containing more than 140 exotic instruments' and careened, as Frank Rich put it, 'from eclectic Eastern folk improvisations to Kabuki percussion to recorded Indian music' (1992). This repertoire of sound borrowings worked, as more traditional theatrical music so often does (think of the *aulos* in the first Greek theatres), to create atmosphere and tension in the plot as well as to shape emotional response in the audience. But it was never made explicit as to why this predominantly non-Western soundscape was crucial to Mnouchkine's re-imagination of canonical Western drama. The appropriation of sound forms, in both *Les Atrides* and other Mnouchkine productions, has not surprisingly generated extensive criticism. Sound (along with costume and acting style) has been justifiably labelled 'Orientalist'.

Linking the soundscapes of intercultural theatre with the global marketing of 'world music', Tan suggests that audiences willingly engage in sonic tourism, even as these performances (both musical and theatrical) have played a part in increasing knowledge of and appetite for work from elsewhere. At the very least, we need to better account for, locate and historicize sound selection in all theatrical productions. At the same time, we must ethically weigh the appropriateness of working to create soundscapes that borrow from cultures other than our own. Moreover, we must remember that what we think sound is and how we think it works comes to us from theories that have evolved within Western intellectual traditions. Sound is, as Sterne describes it, 'an artefact of the messy and political human sphere' (2003: 13) and undoubtedly we need to understand it more inclusively. With such a goal in mind, there is potential in Tan's argument that when 'sounds of various cultural traditions are juxtaposed, adapted, hybridised and reinvented', 'the acoustic texts disclose cultural contestations and conversations' within the intercultural performance (2012: 198). In other words, he suggests that if we take up the opportunity to listen more carefully to the sounds of intercultural performance not just as exotic re-framings of Western theatrical practice, we might find vital entry points into an expanded and more comprehensive attention to sonic cultures.

Across its three sections, *Sound* records the theories and practices of Western performance culture from the Greeks to headphone theatre, but it ends with the acknowledgement that there is much work still to be done in opening up this area of study to 'sonorous enculturated worlds' elsewhere. What 'aural sensibilities' (Samuels et al. 2010: 339) might we bring to understanding sonic environments beyond the West and how would an expanded sound archive inspire new methodologies for a more thoroughly global theatre history and newly diverse theatrical practices? Moreover, even within Western traditions, there are absences and omissions in the theorization of sound. Adrian Curtin has warned against 'making assumptions that are transhistorical, universalist or ableist' (Curtin and Roesner 2015: 121), even as many of the theorists and theatre makers discussed here have done exactly that. How do we as performance scholars determined to follow Irigaray's injunction to ethical listening and move beyond the reverberations of these previously held sonic assumptions?

If this is indeed the age of 'ubiquitous listening' (Kassabian 2013: 40), we still have a very many more places and peoples to hear from.

REFERENCES

Academy of Ancient Music. 'The AAM Story'. Accessed online: http://www.aam.co.uk/#/who-we-are/aam-story.aspx

Aristophanes (1964). *The Wasps, the Poet and the Women, The Frogs*. Harmondsworth: Penguin Book.

Aristotle (2013). *Poetics*. Trans. Anthony Kenny. Oxford: Oxford University Press.

Attali, Jacques (2012). 'Noise: The Political Economy of Music', in Jonathan Sterne (ed.), *The Sound Studies Reader*, 29–39, New York: Routledge.

Bacon, Francis (1651). *Sylva Sylvarum, or, a Natural History in Ten Centuries*. London: J. F. for William Lee.

Barnes Foundation. 'Artist Project: Andrea Hornick: Unbounded Histories'. Accessed online: https://www.barnesfoundation.org/whats-on/andrea-hornick

Barthes, Roland (1985). *The Responsibility of Forms: Critical Essays on Music, Art and Representation*. Trans. Richard Howard. Berkeley and Los Angeles: University of California Press.

Baugh, Christopher (2013). *Theatre, Performance and Technology: The Development and Transformation of Scenography*. Basingstoke: Palgrave Macmillan.

Beckett, Samuel (1971). *Breath and other shorts*. London: Faber.

Beckett, Samuel (1981). *Krapp's Last Tape and other dramatic pieces*. New York: Grove.

Benjamin, Walter (1999). *The Arcades Project*. Trans. Howard Eiland and Kevin McLaughlin. Cambridge, MA and London: Harvard University Press.

Benjamin, Walter (2008). 'The Work of Art in the Age of Mechanical Reproduction', in Neil Badmington and Julia Thomas (eds), *The Routledge Critical and Cultural Theory Reader*, 34–56, London and New York: Routledge.

Blocker, Jane (2015). 'History in the Present Progressive: Sonic Imposture at *The Pedicord Apts*'. *TDR: The Drama Review* 59.4 (T228) Winter: 36–50.

Bloom, Gina (2007). *Voice in Motion: Staging Gender, Shaping Sound in Early Modern England*. Philadelphia: University of Pennsylvania Press.

Booth, Michael (1981). *Victorian Spectacular Theatre: 1850–1910*. London: Routledge.

Booth, Michael (1991). *Theatre in the Victorian Age*. Cambridge: Cambridge University Press.

Brown, Ross (2010). *Sound: A Reader in Theatre Practice*. Basingstoke: Palgrave Macmillan.

British Museum. 'Audio Guide'. Accessed online: http://www.britishmuseum.org/visiting/planning_your_visit/audio_guides.aspx

Brustein, Robert (2004). 'The Past Revisited'. *The New Republic*, 30 August: 25–7.

Bull, Michael (2011). 'The Audio-Visual iPod', in Jonathan Sterne (ed.), *The Sound Studies Reader*, 197–208, New York: Routledge.

Bull, Michael (2013a). 'iPod Culture: The Toxic Pleasure of Audiotopia', in Trevor Pinch and Karin Bijsterveld (eds), *The Oxford Handbook of Sound Studies*, 526–43, Oxford: Oxford University Press.

Bull, Michael, ed. (2013b). *Sound Studies: Volume 1*. New York: Routledge.

Cabanas, Alice (2013). 'A Look Behind the Scenes'. *Arts Professional*, 8 July. Accessed online: https://www.artsprofessional.co.uk/magazine/266/case-study/look-behind-scenes

Cage, John (1961). *Silence*. Middletown, CT: Wesleyan University Press.

Canguilio, Francesco (1970). 'Detonation: A Synthesis of All Modern Theatre'. *TDR: The Drama Review* 15.1 (Autumn): 131.

Cardiff, Janet and George Bures Miller. Accessed online: http://www.cardiffmiller.com/index.html

Carlson, Marvin (1993). *Theories of the Theatre: A Historical and Critical Survey, from the Greeks to the Present*. Expanded edition. Ithaca, NY: Cornell University Press.

Cecchetto, David (2013). *Humanesis: Sound and Technological Posthumanism*. Minneapolis: Minnesota University Press.

Chion, Michel (2012). 'The Three Listening Modes', in Jonathan Sterne (ed.), *The Sound Studies Reader*, 48–53, New York: Routledge.

Chow, Rey and James A. Steintrager (2011). 'In Pursuit of the Object of Sound: An Introduction'. *Differences: A Journal of Feminist Cultural Studies* 22.2–3: 1–9.

Cocteau, Jean (1951). *The Human Voice*. Trans. Carl Wildman. London: Vision Press.

Collins, Karen (2013). *Playing with Sound: A Theory of Interacting with Sound and Music in Video Games*. Cambridge, MA: MIT Press.

Collison, David (2008). *The Sound of Theatre: From the Ancient Greeks to the Modern Digital Age*. Eastbourne: Plasa.

Cox, Christoph and Daniel Warner, eds (2008). *Audio Culture: Readings in Modern Music*. New York: Continuum.

Crook, Tim (1999). *Radio Drama*. London: Routledge.

Crystal, David (2005). *Pronouncing Shakespeare*. Cambridge: Cambridge University Press.

Curtin, Adrian (2014). *Avant-Garde Theatre Sound: Staging Sonic Modernity*. Basingstoke: Palgrave Macmillan.

Curtin, Adrian and David Roesner (2015). 'Sounding Out "the Scenographic Turn": Eight Position Statements'. *Theatre and Performance Design* 1.1–2: 107–25.

Dean, Tacita (2010). 'Merce Cunningham's Last Dance'. *Guardian*, 27 April. Accessed online: https://www.theguardian.com/stage/2010/apr/27/merce-cunningham-tacita-dean

Declercq, Nico F. and Cindy S. A. Dekeyser (2007). 'Acoustic Diffraction Effects at the Hellenistic Amphitheater of Epidaurus: Seat Rows Responsible for the Marvellous Acoustics'. *Journal of the Acoustical Society of America* 121.4 (April): 2011–22.

Derrida, Jacques (1976). *Of Grammatology*. Trans. Gayatri Chakravorty Spivak. Baltimore: The Johns Hopkins University Press.

Dyson, Francis (2013). 'Etheral Transmissions: The "Tele" of Phone', in Michael Bull (ed.), *Sound Studies Volume 1*, 412–29, New York: Routledge.

Ehrick, Christine (2015). 'Vocal Gender and the Gendered Soundscape: At the Intersection of Gender Studies and Sound Studies'. *Sounding Out!* 2 February. Accessed online: https://soundstudiesblog.com/2015/02/02/vocal-gender-and-the-gendered-soundscape-at-the-intersection-of-gender-studies-and-sound-studies/

Escolme, Bridget (2016). 'Costume', in Bruce Smith (ed.), *The Cambridge Guide to the Worlds of Shakespeare, Volume I: Shakespeare's World*, 105–12, Cambridge: Cambridge University Press.

Expect Theatre. 'PlayMe Podcast'. Accessed online: http://www.playmepodcast.com/expect-theatre/

Finer, Ella (2017). 'The Aura of the Aural'. *Performance Research* 22.3: 15–19.

Flint, R. W. (1971). *Marinetti: Selected Writings*. New York: Farrar, Straus and Giroux.

Folkerth, Wes (2002). *The Sound of Shakespeare*. London: Routledge.

Freud, Sigmund (1912). *The Standard Edition of the Complete Psychological Works of Sigmund Freud*, vol. 12. Trans. James Strachey, London: Hogarth Press.

Freud, Sigmund (1930). *The Standard Edition of the Complete Psychological Works of Sigmund Freud*, vol. 21 *(1927–1931)*. Trans. James Strachey, New York: Norton.

Frost, Everett C. (1991). 'Fundamental Sounds: Recording Samuel Beckett's Radio Plays'. *Theatre Journal* 43: 361–76.

Frost, Vicky (2014). 'Situation Rooms by Rimini Protokoll – Review'. *Guardian*, 18 February. Accessed online: https://www.theguardian.com/culture/australia-culture-blog/2014/feb/18/situation-rooms-by-rimini-protokoll-review

Gamel, Mary-Kay (2007). 'Sondheim Floats Frogs', in Edith Hall and Amanda Wrigley (eds), *Aristophanes in Performance 421 BC–AD 2007*, 209–30, London: Modern Humanities Research Association and Maney Publishing.

Gardner, Lyn (2016). 'Reassembled, Slightly Askew Review – Medical Drama Puts Us in Hospital Beds'. *Guardian*, 16 May. Accessed online: https://www.theguardian.com/stage/2016/may/16/reassembled-slightly-askew-review-battersea-arts-centre

Goehr, Lydia (2007). *The Imaginary Museum of Musical Works: An Essay in the Philosophy of Music*. Oxford: Oxford University Press.

Goldhill, Simon (2007). *How to Stage Greek Tragedy Today*. Chicago: University of Chicago Press.

Greenblatt, Stephen (1990). *Learning to Curse: Essays in Early Modern Culture*. New York: Routledge.

Griffith, Mark (2013). *Aristophanes' Frogs*. Oxford: Oxford University Press.

Grimshaw, Mark (2017). 'The Privatisation of Sound Space', in Marcel Cobussen, Vincent Meelberg and Barry Truax (eds), *The Routledge Companion to Sounding Art*, 467–84, New York: Routledge.

Haire, Meaghan (2009). 'The Walkman'. *Time*, 1 July. Accessed online: http://content.time.com/time/nation/article/0,8599,1907884,00.html

Hall, Edith (2002). 'The Singing Actors of Antiquity', in Pat Easterling and Edith Hall (eds), *Greek and Roman Actors: Aspects of an Ancient Profession*, 3–38, Cambridge: Cambridge University Press.

Hermes, Will (2000). 'The Story of 4'33"'. *NPR Music*, 8 May. Accessed online: https://www.npr.org/2000/05/08/1073885/4-33

Home-Cook, George (2015). *Theatre and Aural Attention: Stretching Ourselves*. Basingstoke: Palgrave Macmillan.

Hornick, Andrea. 'Sound Works and Performances > Barnes Foundation Project: Unbounded Histories'. Accessed online: http://andreahornick.squarespace.com/sound-works/barnes-foundation-project-unbounded-histories/

Hosokawa, Shuhei (1984). 'The Walkman Effect'. *Popular Music* 4: 165–80.

Irigaray, Luce (1996). *I Love to You: Sketch of a Possible Felicity in History*. Trans. Alison Martin. New York: Routledge.

Jones, Gwilyn (2013). 'Storm Effects in Shakespeare', in Tiffany Stern and Farah Karim-Cooper (eds), *Shakespeare's Theatre and the Effects of Performance*, 33–50, London: Arden Shakespeare.

Kahn, Douglas (2013). 'Noises of the Avant-Garde', in Michael Bull (ed.), *Sound Studies: Volume 1*, 82–105, New York: Routledge.

Kane, Brian (2014). *Sound Unseen: Acousmatic Sound in Theory and Practice*. Oxford: Oxford University Press.

Kassabian, Anahid (2013). *Ubiquitous Listening: Affect, Attention, and Distributed Subjectivity*. Berkeley: University of California Press.

Kaye, Deena and James Lebrecht (2013). *Sound and Music for the Theatre: The Art and Technique of Design*. 3rd edition. Burlington, MA: Focal Press.

Kendrick, Lynne (2017). *Theatre Aurality*. London: Palgrave Macmillan.

Kendrick, Lynne and David Roesner (2011). *Theatre Noise: The Sound of Performance*. Cambridge: Cambridge Scholars.

Kirby, Michael and Victoria Nes Kirby (1986). *Futurist Performance*. New York: PAJ Publications.

Klich, Rosemary (2017). 'Amplifying Sensory Spaces: The In- and Out-Puts of Headphone Theatre'. *Contemporary Theatre Review* 27.3: 366–78.

Kontomichos, Fotios et al. (2014). 'The Sound Effect of Ancient Greek Theatrical Masks'. *Proceedings ICMC/SMC*. Accessed online: http://quod.lib.umich.edu/cgi/p/pod/dod-idx/sound-effect-of-ancient-greek-theatrical-masks.pdf?c=icmc;idno=bbp2372.2014.220

Kostelanetz, Richard, ed. (1991). *John Cage: An Anthology*. Cambridge, MA: Da Capo.

Leavy, Patricia (2011). *Oral History: Understanding Qualitative Research*. New York: Oxford University Press.

Lehmann, Hans-Thies (2006). *Postdramatic Theatre*. New York: Routledge.

Ley, Graham (2006). *A Short Introduction to the Ancient Greek Theatre*. Chicago: University of Chicago Press.

Ley, Graham (2007). *The Theatricality of Greek Tragedy*. Chicago: University of Chicago Press.

Lindley, David (2008). 'Music, Authenticity and Audience', in Christie Carson and Farah Karim-Cooper (eds), *Shakespeare's Globe: A Theatrical Experiment*, 90–100, Cambridge: Cambridge University Press.

Linley, David (2016). 'Music', in Bruce Smith (ed.), *The Cambridge Guide to the Worlds of Shakespeare, Volume I: Shakespeare's World,* 135–40, Cambridge: Cambridge University Press.

Maina, Claudia (2011). 'The "Scoppiatore". The Intonarumori by Luigi Russolo'. *Digicult 65* (June). Accessed online: http://digicult.it/digimag/issue-065/the-scoppiatore-the-intonarumori-by-luigi-russolo/

Marinetti, Filippo Tommaso (1972). *Selected Writings*. Ed. R. W. Flint. Trans. R. W. Flint and Arthur A. Coppotelli. New York: Farrar, Straus and Giroux.

McMurty, Leslie (2016). 'The Magical Post-Horn: A Trip to the BBC Archive Centre in Perivale'. *Sound Studies*, 26 September. Accessed online: https://soundstudiesblog.com/?s=archive

Meier, Paul (2016). 'Pronunciation and OP on the Modern Stage', in Bruce R. Smith (ed.), *The Cambridge Guide to the Worlds* of Shakespeare: Shakespeare's World, 1500–1660*, 178–83, Cambrdige: Cambridge University Press.

MOLA (Museum of London Archaeology) (2016). "Initial Findings from Excavation at Shakespeare's Curtain Theatre Revealed". 17 May. Accessed online: www.mola.org.uk/blog/initial-findings-excavation-shakespeare%E2%80%99s-curtain-theatre-revealed

Morin, Emilie (2014). 'Beckett's Speaking Machines: Sound, Radiophonics and Acousmatics'. *Modernism/Modernity* 21.1: 1–22.

Morrow, Martin (2011). 'More Visceral than Emotional Truth in "La Voix Humaine"'. *Globe & Mail*, 4 March. Accessed online: https://www.theglobeandmail.com/arts/theatre-and-performance/more-visceral-than-emotional-truth-in-la-voix-humaine/article628013/

Muller, Julie (1994), 'Music as Meaning in *The Tempest*', in A. J. Hoenselaars (ed.), *Reclamations of Shakespeare*, 187–200, Amsterdam: Rodopi.

Neumark, Norie (2017). 'Voicing Memories'. *Sound Effects: An Interdisciplinary Journal of Sound and Sound Experience* 7.2: 32–44.

Nyman, Michael (2008). 'Towards (a Definition of) Experimental Music', in Christoph Cox and Daniel Warner (eds), *Audio Culture: Readings in Modern Music*, 209–20, New York: Continuum.

Open University (2011). 'Shakespeare: Original Pronunciation'. Accessed online: https://www.youtube.com/watch?v=gPlpphT7n9s

Ovadija, Mladen (2016). *Dramaturgy of Sound in the Avant-Garde and Postdramatic Theatre*. Montreal: McGill-Queens University Press.

Pavis, Patrice (2003). *Analyzing Performance: Theater, Dance, and Film*. Trans. David Williams. Ann Arbor: The University of Michigan Press.

Petralia, Peter Salvatore (2014). 'Headspace: Architectural Space in the Brain'. *Contemporary Theatre Review* 20.1: 96–108.

Pinch, Trevor and Karin Bijsterveld (2012). 'New Keys to the World of Sound', in Trevor Pinch and Karin Bijsterveld (eds), *The Oxford Handbook of Sound Studies*, 3–35, Oxford: Oxford University Press.

'Playback: 130-Year-Old Sounds Revealed' (2011). *Newsdesk: Newsroom of the Smithsonian*, 14 December. Accessed online:

https://newsdesk.si.edu/releases/playback-130-year-old-sounds-revealed

Porter, Jeff (2010). 'Samuel Beckett and the Radiophonic Body: Beckett and the BBC'. *Modern Drama* 53.4 (Winter): 431–46.

Radcliffe, Allan (2016). 'Theatre: The Suppliant Women, Royal Lyceum, Edinburgh'. *Times*, 7 October. Accessed online: https://www.thetimes.co.uk/article/theatre-the-suppliant-women-royal-lyceum-edinburgh-sq9k9d63f

Rainey, Lawrence et al., eds (2009). *Futurism: An Anthology*. New Haven, CT: Yale University Press.

Reassembled, Slightly Askew. Accessed online: http://reassembled.co.uk/welcome

Reidy, Brent Karpfet al. (2016). *Live-to-Digital: Understanding the Immpact of Digital Developments in Theatre on Audiences, Production and Distribution*. Aeaconsulting.com.

Rice, Tom (2015). 'Listening', in David Novak and Matt Sakkakeeny (eds), *Keywords in Sound*, 99–111, Durham, NC: Duke University Press.

Rich, Frank (1992). 'Review/Theater: Les Atrides, Taking the Stage to Some of Its Extremes'. *New York Times*, 6 October. Accessed online: https://www.nytimes.com/1992/10/06/theater/review-theater-les-atrides-taking-the-stage-to-some-of-its-extremes.html

Russolo, Luigi (2013). 'The Art of Noise: Futurist Manifesto', in Michael Bull (ed.), *Sound Studies: Volume 1*, 75–81, New York: Routledge.

Samuels, David W., Louise Meintjes, Ana Maria Ochoa and Thomas Porcello (2010). 'Soundscapes: Toward a Sounded Anthropology'. *Annual Review of Anthropology* 39: 329–45.

Schaeffer, Pierre (2008). 'Acousmatics', in Christoph Cox and Daniel Warner (eds), *Audio Culture: Readings in Modern Music*, 76–81, New York: Continuum.

Schaeffer, Pierre (2017). *Treatise on Musical Objects: An Essay across Disciplines*. Trans. Christine North and John Dack. Berkeley: University of California Press.

Schafer, R. Murray (2008). 'The Music of the Environment', in Christoph Cox and Daniel Warner (eds), *Audio Culture: Readings in Modern Music*, 29–39, New York: Continuum.

Sellars, Peter (1992). 'Foreword', in Deena Kaye and James Lebrecht (eds), *Sound and Music for the Theatre: The Art and Technique of Design*, 3rd edition, Burlington, MA: Focal Press.

Shakespeare, William (2011). *The Tempest*. Eds Alden T. Vaughan and Virginia Mason Vaughan. London: Arden Shakespeare.

Shanahan, John (2013). 'The Dryden-Davenant *Tempest*, Wonder Production, and the State of Natural Philosophy in 1667'. *The Eighteenth-Century* 54.1: 91–118.

Siddall, Gillian and Ellen Waterman, eds (2016). *Negotiated Moments: Improvisation, Sound and Subjectivity*. Durham, NC and London: Duke University Press.

Smith, Bruce R. (1999). *The Acoustic World of Early Modern England*. Chicago: University of Chicago Press.

Smith, Bruce R. (2004). 'Listening to the Wild Blue Yonder: The Challenges of Acoustic Ecology', in Veit Erlmann (ed.), *Hearing Cultures: Essays on Sound, Listening and Modernity*, 21–43, Oxford: Berg Publishers.

Smith, Bruce R. (2013). 'Within, Without, Withinwards: The Circulation of Sound in Shakespeare's Theatre', in Tiffany Stern and Farah Karim-Cooper (eds), *Shakespeare's Theatres and the Effects of Performance*, 171–94, London: Arden Shakespeare.

Stadler, Gustavus (2010a). 'Introduction: Breaking Sound Barriers'. *Social Text* 28.1 (102): 1–12.

Stadler, Gustavus (2010b). 'Never Heard Such a Thing: Lynching and Phonographic Modernity'. *Social Text* 28.1 (102): 87–105.

Stein, Gertrude (1957). *Lectures in America*. Boston, MA: Beacon Press.

Stern, Tiffany (2013). '"This Wide and Universal Theatre": The Theatre as Prop in Shakespeare's Metadrama', in Tiffany Stern and Farah Karim-Cooper (eds), *Shakespeare's Theatres and the Effects of Performance*, 11–32, London: Arden Shakespeare.

Stern, Tiffany (2015). '"Before the Beginning; After the End": When Did Plays Start and Stop', in M. J. Kidnie and Sonia Massai (eds), *Shakespeare and Textual Studies*, 358–74, Cambridge: Cambridge University Press.

Sterne, Jonathan (2003). *The Audible Past: Cultural Origins of Sound Reproduction*. Durham, NC and London: Duke University Press.

Sterne, Jonathan (2012). 'Sonic Imaginations', in Jonathan Sterne (ed.), *The Sound Studies Reader*, 1–17, New York and London: Routledge.

Stoever, J. L. (2009). 'The Grain of the Voice or the Contour of the Ear?' *Sounding Out!* 15 September. Accessed online: https://

soundstudiesblog.com/2009/09/15/the-grain-of-the-voice-or-the-contour-of-the-ear/

Tan, Marcus Cheng Chye (2012). *Acoustic Interculturalism: Listening to Performance*. Basingstoke: Palgrave Macmillan.

Thompson, Emily (2002). *The Soundscape of Modernity: Architectural Acoustics and the Culture of Listening in America*. Cambridge, MA: MIT Press.

Tubridy, Derval (2007). 'Sounding Spaces: Aurality in Samuel Beckett, Janet Cardiff and Bruce Nauman'. *Performance Research* 12.1: 5–11.

Van Drie, Melissa (2015). 'Hearing through the *Théâtrephone*: Sonically Constructed Spaces and Embodied Listening in Late Nineteenth-Century French Theatre'. *Sound Effects: An Interdisciplinary Journal of Sound and Sound Experience* 5.1: 74–90.

Van Kampen, Claire (2008). 'Music and Aural Texture at Shakespeare's Globe', in Christie Carson and Farah Karim-Cooper (eds), *Shakespeare's Globe: A Theatrical Experiment*, 79–89, Cambridge: Cambridge University Press.

Vitruvius (1999). *Ten Books on Architecture*. Eds Ingrid D. Rowland and Thomas Noble Howe. Cambridge: Cambridge University Press.

Voegelin, Salomé (2010). *Listening to Noise and Silence: Towards a Philosophy of Sound Art*. New York: Continuum.

Walraven, Maarten (2013). 'History and Its Acoustic Context: Silence, Resonance, Echo and Where to Find Them in the Archive'. *Journal of Sonic Studies* 4.1 (May). Accessed online: http://journal.sonicstudies.org/vol04/nr01/a07

Warden, Claire (2015). *Modernist and Avant-Garde Performance*. Edinburgh: Edinburgh University Press.

Weingust, Don (2014). 'Authentic Performances or Performances of Authenticity? Original Practices and the Repertory Schedule'. *Shakespeare* 10.4: 402–10.

Wenn, Chris (2015). 'Headphone Listening in Live Performance: A Phenomenology of Sound Design'. *Theatre and Performance Design* 1.3: 236–55.

Wilson, Peter (2002). 'The musicians among the actors', in Pat Easterling and Edith Hall (eds), Greek and Roman Actors: Aspects of an Ancient Profession, 39–68, Cambridge: Cambridge University Press.

FURTHER READING

If you would like to explore further, here are some key texts to help you make a start.

Sound and theatre

Ross Brown's *Sound: A Reader in Theatre Practice* (Basingstoke: Palgrave Macmillan, 2010) offers an excellent introduction to thinking about sound in a theatre setting, with particular interest in elements of sound design practice. Another key volume on practical approaches to sound design is Deena Kaye and James Lebrecht, *Sound and Music for the Theatre: The Art and Technique of Design* (Burlington, MA: Focal Press, 2009 – 3rd ed.).

David Collison's *The Sound of Theatre: From the Ancient Greeks to the Modern Digital Age* (Eastbourne: Plasa, 2008) is chiefly a discussion of sound recording and amplification, but the author precedes that work with a brief and introductory history of mechanical sound effects and a chronology of those inventions that made sound recording and amplification possible.

Lynne Kendrick's *Theatre Aurality* (London: Palgrave Macmillan, 2017) is concerned with the theories and phenomenologies of sound, explored through a series of case studies of contemporary performances. Students interested in more phenomenological/philosophical approaches to thinking about sound will also benefit from Jean-Luc Nancy's *Listening* (New York: Fordham University Press, 2007) and Peter Szendy's *Listen: A History of Our Ears* (New York: Fordham University Press, 2008) – both translated by Charlotte Mandell.

Ranging across theories from phenomenology to post-structuralism, Andrew M. Kimbrough's *Dramatic Theories of Voice in the Twentieth Century* (Amherst, NY: Cambria Press, 2011) connects this multiplicity of perspectives with diverse theatrical examples of voice from Artaud to the Wooster Group.

Adrian Curtin's *Avant-Garde Theatre Sound: Staging Sonic Modernity* (London: Palgrave Macmillan, 2014) is an important and engaging monograph that provides a theoretically sophisticated study of the importance of sound in experimental performance of the late nineteenth and early twentieth centuries. The book has an extensive bibliography that would prove useful to anyone thinking specifically about performance in the Modern period.

Theatre and Performance Design (Routledge) publishes essays that often work between critical and practical perspectives. Volume 2, issues 3–4, edited by Adrian Curtin and David Roesner, specifically addresses sound ('Sounds Good') and has a rich collection of essays with thought-provoking case study examples. *Performance Research* 15.3 (2010), edited by Catherine Laws, is titled 'On Listening' and examines the topic in the context of performance, performativity and embodied process. A CD is included as part of the issue.

A special issue of Critical Stages/Scénes critiques on 'sound/Theatre: Sound in Performance' (volume 16, December 2017), available online and edited by Johannes Birringer, offers eleven essays on a range of sound practices across performance disciplines. Embedded videos make this a particularly rich collection.

Interdisciplinary sound studies

David Novak and Matt Sakkakeeny's edited volume *Keywords in Sound* (Durham, NC: Duke University Press, 2015) is a useful resource for further study on terminology and to locate related bibliography: 'This book is a conceptual lexicon of specific keywords that cut across the material and metaphorical lives of sound' (2015: 2).

Sounding Out! is an online interdisciplinary Sound Studies journal (https://soundstudiesblog.com/), indexed by the Modern Language Association. The journal is key term searchable (includes 'drama', 'soundscape', 'soundwalk'). They also publish a regular podcast that covers sound walks, sound art, lectures by leading scholars and other sound-related topics (https://soundstudiesblog.com/episode-guide/).

Sound Effects: An Interdisciplinary Journal of Sound and Sound Experience (https://www.soundeffects.dk) is open access and online.

Other resources

The Sound Book Project, performances created by a collective of artists and musicians using books as instruments (https://www.soundbookproject.com/).

Centuries of Sound (https://centuriesofsound.wordpress.com/about/) aims to produce an audio mix in MP3 format for every year of recorded sound, from 1859–60 to the present. As of October 2018, the project is completed only until 1907 but the plan is to release a new year on the first of every month (free to subscribe as a podcast). While most of the material is not surprisingly period music and songs, there are also scenes and speeches from plays, lectures and everyday sounds. The mix for 1890 includes Edwin Booth (from *Othello*) and 1892 an extract from the Peking Opera. The project's ambition to be global in its sweep is impressive, evident even in the materials chosen to represent the first years of recorded sound.

The website of the American Professional organization TSDCA (Theatrical Sound Designers and Composers Association) has a wealth of educational materials as well as news of upcoming events. There are key materials on equity, diversity and inclusion that deserve attention, viewed alongside Elizabeth Freestone's report on UK theatres (see page 111).

INDEX

Academy of Ancient Music 29, 31
acoustics 4, 15, 24, 32–3, 103
   acousmatic experience 81
   acousmatics 6, 79, 81
   acousmatic voice 91
   acoustical science 16, 26
   acoustic archaeology 6, 9, 51, 89
   acoustic consciousness 59
   acoustic ecology 99
   acoustic environment 97, 98, 112 (*see also* environment; sound, sonic environment)
   acoustic interculturalism 129
   acoustic properties 36
Actors Company, The 21, 23, 51
Ader, Clément 64
Aeschylus 19, 21–3, 129
   Agamemnon 19
   Eumenides 19
   Suppliant Women, The 21, 23, 29, 51
affect 3, 11, 59, 86, 87, 91, 106, 114, 117, 124
ancient Greece 6, 15–24, 49, 51. *See also* Greek tragedy
anechoic chamber 73, 77, 101
architecture 27, 105. *See also* aurality, aural architecture

Aristophanes 11, 21
   The Frogs 11, 21–3
Aristotle 15, 17–18, 20–1
   Poetics 15, 17–18
Attali, Jacques 9, 10
audience 5, 8, 17, 55, 57, 61, 65, 67, 72, 76, 77, 79, 95, 97, 101, 106, 109, 118, 121, 127
audio and audio-video walks 63, 70, 102–7, 110, 113, 120, 124
audio guide 107–12, 127
aulos 20, 21, 130
aura 87, 88
aurality 4
   aural architecture 24–6, 36, 50
   aural attention 5

Bacon, Francis 27, 32–5, 99
   Sylva Sylvarum 27, 32–5
Barenaked Ladies 41
Barnes Foundation 108–11
Barthes, Roland 9–10, 19–20, 21, 51, 67, 68–9, 70, 73–4
Battersea Arts Centre 117
Baugh, Christopher 94
Beck, Julian 75
Beckett, Samuel 6, 11, 77, 78–9, 81–4, 90–3
   All That Fall 81–4
   'Breath' 77–8, 115

Endgame 84
Krapp's Last Tape 11, 84, 88, 90–3
Bell, Alexander Graham 86, 89
Benjamin, Walter 60, 87–8, 101
Beyoncé 70
Bijsterveld, Karin 1, 8
binaural recording 105, 114–15, 117, 118
Blackfriars Playhouse (Staunton, VA) 27
Blocker, Jane 91
Bloom, Gina 37, 45
Bluetooth technology 113, 120, 127
Booth, Edwin 90
Booth, Michael 51–2
Borelli, Lydia 61–2
Bovy, Berthe 65
Brendemühl, Jutta 123
British Broadcasting Corporation (BBC) 63, 78–9, 81, 82, 83, 84, 90
British Museum 107–8
Brown, Ross 5, 7, 73
Browne, John 21
Bruitism 62
Buchelius, Arnoldus 37
Bull, Michael 1, 12, 95, 127
Burdett, Samuel 85–7

Cage, John 11, 62, 70–8, 98, 101
'4'33"' 71–4, 76, 102
'Water Music' 71
Cangiulio, Francesco 55
'*Detonazione*' 55
Cardiff, Janet 12, 70, 102–7, 109, 114, 121, 124, 127
'Forest Walk' 12, 102–5

'The Missing Voice: Case Study B' 105
'The Telephone Call' 12, 70, 105–7
Cecchetto, David 2
Chamber, Iain 101
Chion, Michel 6
chorus 18, 20, 21, 22, 43
Chow, Rey 5
City Dionysia 17, 21
Cocteau, Jean 11, 65–70, 76
  The Human Voice 11, 65–70, 76, 84, 92, 105, 107
Collins, Karen 102, 121
Collison, David 26, 52, 63
Comédie-Française 64, 65, 85
Cornford, Tom 30
Corr, Bruno 55
Corsetti, Giorgio Barberio 45
  La Tempesta 45
Crook, Tim 78
Crystal, Ben 30–1
Crystal, David 30–1, 50
Cunningham, Merce 76
Curtin, Adrian 53, 57, 62, 67, 131

Dada 62
Davenant, William 48
Dean, Tacita 76
Declercq, Nico F. 15–16, 24
de Forest, Lee 64
Deleuze, Gilles 100, 108, 111
Dekeyser, Cindy S.A. 15–16, 24
Derrida, Jacques 92–3
De Witt, Johannes 37
Dionysus 21–3
Doctor Who 83
Dolmetsch, Arnold 28
Dryden, John 48

echea 26
Ehrick, Christine 111
embodiment 2, 7, 101, 112, 116, 117, 123–4, 126
environment 7, 41, 50, 55, 57, 71, 72, 76, 98, 104, 105, 118, 127. See also acoustics, acoustic environment; sound, sonic environment
Epidaurus 10, 15–16, 24
ethics 120, 122, 125, 130. See also listening, ethical listening
Euripides 19, 21–3, 129
Expect Theatre 1
Expressionism 62

Fanon, Frantz 128
Finer, Ella 66
Folkerth, Wes 36
Freestone, Elizabeth 111
Freud, Sigmund 63, 65, 68
Frost, Everett 83
Frost, Vicky 122, 126
Futurism 11, 54, 57, 58, 59, 60, 62, 66, 71, 75. See also Italian Futurists

Gardner, Lyn 117
Garrick, David 48
gender 111, 112, 125
Goehr, Lydia 31
Goldenthal, Elliot 47
Goldhill, Simon 19
Gough, Orlando 41
gramophone 54, 78. See also phonograph
gramophone record 81
Greek tragedy 16–19

Greenblatt, Stephen 45
Griffith, Mark 17, 22
Grimshaw, Mark 3, 11
Guattari, Félix 100, 108, 110–11

Haartsen, Jaap 113
Hall, Edith 16–17
Handel, George Frideric 71
Harvard University 73
Haug, Helgard Kim 119, 120, 121
headphones 1, 10, 12, 63, 99–100, 105, 113, 117, 119, 120, 122, 123, 127
  headphone theatre 63, 84, 87, 97, 102, 107, 114–19, 125, 127, 131
High Performance Rodeo festival (Calgary) 115
Hirsch, Nikolaus 121
Hirst, Damien 78
Home-Cook, George 5–6
Hornick, Andrea 107–12, 127
Hosokawa, Shuhei 100–2, 113
Husserl, Edmund 80, 81

Ibsen, Henrik 75
intonamuri 11, 57–8, 61, 62
iPad 120, 122
iPod 1, 70, 95
Irigaray, Luce 107, 112, 125, 131
Irving, Sir Henry 90
Italian Futurists 11, 54–62, 69

Jones, Gwilyn 39, 42
Journal of the Acoustical Society of America, The 15

INDEX

Kaegi, Stefan 119, 120, 121
Kane, Brian 81
Kassabian, Anahid 2
Kaye, Deena 7
Kean, Charles 48
Kendrick, Lynne 4, 94
kinesonic synchresis 121, 123
Klich, Rosemary 97, 117, 118
Kyd, Thomas 35
   The Spanish Tragedy 35

Lane, Nathan 23
Law, Arthur 52
   The Judge 52
Leachman, Silas 86
Leavy, Patricia 113
Lebrecht, James 7
Le Figaro 54
Lehmann, Hans-Thies 4
Lemetre, Jean Jacques 129–30
Lennon, John 78
Lewis, Wyndham 56
Ley, Graham 17, 18–19
Linley, David 29, 38–40
listening 5, 6, 8, 9, 10, 12, 20, 33–4, 44–5, 58, 67, 68–9, 70, 73–4, 81, 86, 90, 93, 94, 99–101, 111, 113, 117, 121, 123, 125
   akroasis 16
   concentrated listening 99, 101
   deterritorialised listening 100
   ethical listening 112, 114, 118, 129, 131
   focused listening 62
   headphone listening 1, 99, 112, 118 (*see also* headphones)
   reduced listening 81, 84
   role of listener 3, 24, 65, 79, 104
   ubiquitous listening 2, 131
liveness 64, 105
Living Theater, The 75
Lucy, Martha 109
Luminato Festival (Toronto) 122

machines 52, 58, 61, 64, 71
   sea machine 42
   wind machine 42
Malina, Judith 75
Marinetti, Filippo Tomaso 54–62, 63, 66, 72
   Il Tamburo di Fuoco 62
   'The Founding and Manifesto of Futurism' 54
   'The Futurist Synthetic Theatre' 55, 56
   Zong Toomb Toomb 56
Marling, Laura 41
masks 16
Maverick Concert Hall 71–2
McWhinnie, Donald 82, 84
Meier, Paul 29
memory 3, 11, 80, 93, 117–18
Merce Cunningham Dance Company 75
Mirren, Helen 47
Mnouchkine, Ariane 129
   Les Atrides 129–30
modernity 53–4, 60–1, 63, 76
Morin, Emilie 84
Morley, Thomas 41
Muller, Julie 48
music 1, 4, 7, 8, 10, 17, 19–21, 28–9, 32, 40–1, 43, 46–8, 52, 58, 69, 71–5, 82, 98

echo music 48
music gallery 27–8
musique concrete 81, 98
world music 130

National Museum of American History 89
National Theatre (London) 41, 64
Neumark, Norie 104
Newell, Anna 114
Night at the Museum 110
Ninagawa, Yukio 129
noise 1, 4, 8, 42, 46, 47, 49, 53, 57, 58, 60, 71, 75, 76, 94, 98. See also Russolo, Luigi
notation, musical 74

ocularcentrism 9, 53, 69, 120
O'Farrell, Mary 83
Ovadija, Mladen 4

pantomimi 34, 44
Pavis, Patrice 7, 8
Pentabus Theatre 111
Pepys, Samuel 48
Petralia, Peter Salvatore 107
phenomenology 5, 80
Philpott, Lachlan 118
phonograph 52, 63, 85. See also gramophone
phonograph records 87, 89–90
Pinch, Trevor 1, 8
'PlayMe' podcast 1, 84
Poel, William 28
Porter, Jeff 83
Pratella, Balilla 58
pronunciation, original 29

Punchdrunk 57
Sleep No More 57
Pythagoras 79

Radcliffe, Allan 21
radio 64, 71, 75, 78, 79, 81
radio play 78, 81–4, 114, 120
Radiodiffusion-Télévision Française 82
Rauschenberg, Robert 76
Rawley, William 32
realism 52
Reijn, Halina 69
resonance 4, 26, 49, 50
rhythm 7, 17, 22, 95
Rich, Frank 130
Rimini Protokoll 12, 113
Situation Rooms 12, 113, 119–26
Royal Court Theatre 84
Royal Shakespeare Company 30, 41
Russolo, Luigi 11, 57–62, 63, 98
'The Art of Noise' 57–61

San Francisco Museum of Modern Art 105, 106
Schaeffer, Pierre 6, 78–81, 82, 91, 98
Schafer, R. Murray 76, 97–100, 102, 112
Scientific American 54, 63
Scott, A.O. 47
Sellars, Peter 3–4, 94–5
Sen, Ong Keng 129
Settimelli, Emilio 55
Shakespeare, William 4, 11, 19, 23, 47, 59, 75, 90
As You Like It 41
Cymbeline 23

Hamlet 29, 35, 38, 40, 63, 89
Julius Caesar 39
King Henry VI, Part 2 38
King Henry VI, Part 3 38
Macbeth 38
The Merchant of Venice 40
Othello 38
Romeo and Juliet 30, 40
The Taming of the Shrew 39
The Tempest 4, 11, 33, 41–8
Titus Andronicus 38
Troilus and Cressida 30
Twelfth Night 38, 90
Shakespeare's Globe 10, 27–31, 50, 99
Shaw, George Bernard 23
Shepard, Sam 78
Siddall, Gillian 112
silence 4, 49, 67, 71, 73, 76, 77, 79, 93, 94, 112, 116, 117
Silent Disco 127
Smith, Bruce R. 6, 9, 28, 36–8, 39, 49, 51, 59, 99
Sondheim, Stephen 23
song 4, 17, 19–21, 41, 43–4, 47
Sony Walkman. *See* Walkman
Sophocles 19
sound
  archive 49, 84, 85, 88–90, 104, 131
  definition 3, 35
  sonic adaptation 20
  sonic environment 48, 49, 53, 76, 117 (*see also* acoustics, acoustic environment; environment)
  sonic *flâneur* 60
  sonic history 7, 29, 31
  sonic imagination 10, 48–52, 65, 117

  sonic scene-setting 39
  sonic tourism 130
  sonic turn 2
  sonorous object 80–2, 83
  sound effects 4, 10, 43, 52, 62, 82, 94, 106
  sound poem 56, 109
  sound recording 52, 54, 63, 77, 78, 83, 84, 85, 87, 88, 98, 129
  soundscape 6–7, 11, 12, 36, 42, 44, 57, 69, 75, 82, 97–8, 100, 103, 104, 107, 114, 118, 124, 126, 128, 129
  soundtrack 1, 2, 4, 29, 62, 109, 116
Stadler, Gustavus 9, 85–7
Stapleton, Paul 114
Stein, Gertrude 2, 12, 76
Steintrager, James A. 5
Stern, Tiffany 37–8
Sterne, Jonathan 8, 9, 48–9, 65, 85, 87–9, 93, 108, 130
Stoever, J.L. 6
Stowe, Harriet Beecher 86
Stratford Festival (Ontario) 41
Streep, Meryl 23
Stroman, Susan 23
surveillance 10

Tan, Marcus Cheng Chye 129, 130
tape recorder 11, 63, 78, 84, 90–3
Taymor, Julie 47
telephone 11, 63–70, 78, 85, 105–6
  mobile phone 76, 106, 109, 113, 115
Terry, Ellen 90

théâtrephone 64, 85
thunder 26, 39, 42, 43, 44, 46, 48
Toneelgroep Amsterdam 69
Tree, Herbert Beerbohm 90
Tudor, David 71
Turbidy, Derval 93
Tynan, Kenneth 77–8
   O! Calcutta! 77–8

Van Drie, Melissa 64–5
van Hove, Ivo 69, 70
van Kampen, Claire 27–8
Vaughan, Alden T. 42
Vaughan, Virginia Mason 42
Versweyveld, Jan 69–70
visuality 2, 9, 31, 69
Vitruvius (Marcus Vitruvius Pollio) 24–6, 36, 49
   De Architectura 24–6
Vivian Beaumont Theatre 23
Vogelin, Salomé 74
voice 4, 7, 17, 19, 24–5, 34–5, 36–7, 54, 68, 70

Walkman (Sony) 12, 100–3, 113, 127
Walraven, Martin 12, 49–50, 51, 90
Walter Phillips Gallery, Banff Centre 102, 104
Wanamaker Theatre 27
Warden, Claire 56
Waterman, Ellen 112
Watson, Thomas 85
Weaver, Sigourney 23
Weber, John S. 106
Weingust, Don 31
Wenn, Christ 117–18
Wetzel, Daniel 119, 120, 121
Williams, Tennessee 75
Wilson, Peter 20–1
World Soundscape Project 98–9

Yale Repertory Theatre 23
Yee, Shannon 12, 73, 113, 114, 116, 124
   Reassembled, Slightly Askew 12, 73, 113, 114–19, 123